Chapter 2
Solving Equations

All-In-One
Teaching Resources

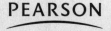

PEARSON

Boston, Massachusetts   Upper Saddle River, New Jersey

ISBN-13: 978-0-13-368916-7
ISBN-10:   0-13-368916-6
3 4 5 6 7 8 9 10   V084   13 12 11 10

Contents

Chapter 2   **Solving Equations**

2-1	ELL	1
2-1	Think About a Plan	2
2-1	Practice Form G	3–4
2-1	Practice Form K	5–6
2-1	Standardized Test Prep	7
2-1	Enrichment	8
2-1	Reteaching	9–10
2-2	ELL	11
2-2	Think About a Plan	12
2-2	Practice Form G	13–14
2-2	Practice Form K	15–16
2-2	Standardized Test Prep	17
2-2	Enrichment	18
2-2	Reteaching	19–20
2-3	ELL	21
2-3	Think About a Plan	22
2-3	Practice Form G	23–24
2-3	Practice Form K	25–26
2-3	Standardized Test Prep	27
2-3	Enrichment	28
2-3	Reteaching	29–30
2-4	ELL	31
2-4	Think About a Plan	32
2-4	Practice Form G	33–34
2-4	Practice Form K	35–36
2-4	Standardized Test Prep	37
2-4	Enrichment	38
2-4	Reteaching	39–40
2-5	ELL	41
2-5	Think About a Plan	42
2-5	Practice Form G	43–44
2-5	Practice Form K	45–46
2-5	Standardized Test Prep	47
2-5	Enrichment	48
2-5	Reteaching	49–50
2-6	ELL	51
2-6	Think About a Plan	52
2-6	Practice Form G	53–54
2-6	Practice Form K	55–56
2-6	Standardized Test Prep	57
2-6	Enrichment	58
2-6	Reteaching	59–60

2-7	ELL	61
2-7	Think About a Plan	62
2-7	Practice Form G	63–64
2-7	Practice Form K	65–66
2-7	Standardized Test Prep	67
2-7	Enrichment	68
2-7	Reteaching	69–70
2-8	ELL	71
2-8	Think About a Plan	72
2-8	Practice Form G	73–74
2-8	Practice Form K	75–76
2-8	Standardized Test Prep	77
2-8	Enrichment	78
2-8	Reteaching	79–80
2-9	ELL	81
2-9	Think About a Plan	82
2-9	Practice Form G	83–84
2-9	Practice Form K	85–86
2-9	Standardized Test Prep	87
2-9	Enrichment	88
2-9	Reteaching	89–90
2-10	ELL	91
2-10	Think About a Plan	92
2-10	Practice Form G	93–94
2-10	Practice Form K	95–96
2-10	Standardized Test Prep	97
2-10	Enrichment	98
2-10	Reteaching	99–100
Chapter 2 Quiz 1 Form G		101
Chapter 2 Quiz 2 Form G		102
Chapter 2 Test Form G		103–104
Chapter 2 Part A Test Form K		105–106
Chapter 2 Part B Test Form K		107–108
Performance Tasks		109–110
Chapter 2 Cumulative Review		111–112
Chapter 2 Project Teacher Notes		113
Chapter 2 Project		114–115
Chapter 2 Project Manager		116
Answers		117–145

2-1 ELL Support

Solving One-Step Equations

Two numbers with a sum equal to zero

☐☐☐ + ■■■ = 0

$3 + (-3) = 0$

Opposites are additive inverses.

Sample 12 and -12 are additive inverses.

Solve.

1. $-32 + 32 = $ ☐

2. Circle the *additive inverse* of 6. -6 $-\frac{1}{6}$ $\frac{1}{6}$ 6

3. Circle the *additive inverse* of -18. -18 $-\frac{1}{18}$ $\frac{1}{18}$ 18

4. Circle the *opposite* of 91. -91 $-\frac{1}{91}$ $\frac{1}{91}$ 91

5. Cross out the pairs of numbers that are NOT *additive inverses*.

27 and -27 4 and -4 10 and 12 $\frac{2}{7}$ and $-\frac{2}{7}$ 15 and 11

Two numbers with a product equal to zero

$4 \times \frac{1}{4} = 1$ $4 \times 0.25 = 1$

Reciprocals are multiplicative inverses.

Sample 4 and $\frac{1}{4}$ are multiplicative inverses.

Solve.

6. $\frac{3}{7} \times \frac{7}{3} = $ ☐

7. Cross out the pairs of numbers that are NOT *multiplicative inverses*.

$\frac{3}{4}$ and $\frac{4}{3}$ $\frac{4}{7}$ and 47 $\frac{9}{5}$ and $\frac{5}{9}$ 6 and $\frac{1}{6}$ 0.1 and 10

8. Circle the *multiplicative inverse* of 6. -6 $-\frac{1}{6}$ $\frac{1}{6}$ 6

9. Circle the *reciprocal* of -18. -18 $-\frac{1}{18}$ $\frac{1}{18}$ 188

2-1 Think About a Plan

Solving One-Step Equations

Volleyball In volleyball, players serve the ball to the opposing team. If the opposing team fails to hit the ball, the service is called an ace. A player's ace average is the number of aces served divided by the number of games played. A certain player has an ace average of 0.3 and has played in 70 games this season. How many aces has the player served?

Understanding the Problem

1. What values are you given?

_____

_____

Planning the Solution

2. Write an expression, using words, to represent the relationship between ace average, number of aces, and the number of games played.

$$\text{Ace Average} = \frac{\boxed{}}{\boxed{}}$$

3. Use the expression to write an equation, where A = number of aces.

$$\boxed{} = \frac{\boxed{}}{\boxed{}}$$

Getting an Answer

4. Solve the equation you wrote in Step 3.

5. Explain what this solution represents.

_____

_____

6. Is your answer reasonable? Explain.

_____

_____

2-1

Practice

Form G

Solving One-Step Equations

Solve each equation using addition or subtraction. Check your answer.

1. $8 = a - 2$

2. $x + 7 = 11$

3. $r - 2 = -6$

4. $-18 = m + 12$

5. $f + 10 = -10$

6. $-1 = n + 5$

Solve each equation using multiplication or division. Check your answer.

7. $-3p = -48$

8. $-98 = 7t$

9. $-4.4 = -4y$

10. $2.8c = 4.2$

11. $\frac{k}{6} = 8$

12. $16 = \frac{w}{8}$

13. $-9 = \frac{y}{-3}$

14. $\frac{h}{10} = \frac{-22}{5}$

Solve each equation. Check your answer.

15. $\frac{3}{5}n = 12$

16. $-4 = \frac{2}{3}b$

17. $\frac{5}{8}x = -15$

18. $\frac{1}{4}z = \frac{2}{5}$

19. Jeremy mowed several lawns to earn money for camp. After he paid $17 for gas, he had $75 leftover to pay towards camp. Write and solve an equation to find how much money Jeremy earned mowing lawns.

2-1

Practice (continued)

Solving One-Step Equations

Define a variable and write an equation for each situation. Then solve.

20. Susan's cell phone plan allows her to use 950 minutes per month with no additional charge. She has 188 minutes left for this month. How many minutes has she already used this month?

21. In the fifth year of operation, the profit of a company was 3 times the profit it earned in the first year of operation. If its profit was $114,000 in the fifth year of operation, what was the profit in the first year?

Solve each equation. Check your answer.

22. $-9x = 48$

23. $-\frac{7}{8} = \frac{2}{3} + n$

24. $a + 1\frac{1}{4} = 2\frac{7}{10}$

25. $-7t = 5.6$

26. $2.3 = -7.9 + y$

27. $\frac{5}{3}p = \frac{8}{3}$

28. $\frac{g}{8} = -\frac{3}{4}$

29. $\frac{m}{8} = 8\frac{1}{3}$

30. A community center is serving a free meal to senior citizens. The center plans to feed 700 people in 4 hours.
   a. Write and solve an equation to find the average number of people the center is planning to feed each hour.

   b. During the first hour and a half, the center fed 270 people. Write and solve an equation to find the number of people that remain to be fed.

2-1

Practice

Solving One-Step Equations

Solve each equation using addition or subtraction. Check your answer.

1. $6 = p - 8$

2. $z + 5 = 4$

3. $m - 4 = 12$

4. $-10 = h - 4$

5. $n + 14 = -5$

6. $2 = a + 7$

Solve each equation using multiplication or division. Check your answer.

7. $4t = -32$

8. $-25 = -5x$

9. $-3.2k = 16$

10. $2.8r = 16.8$

11. $\frac{m}{7} = 4$

12. $25 = \frac{z}{-4}$

Solve each equation. Check your answer.

13. $\frac{3}{4}b = 15$

14. $-8 = \frac{2}{5}t$

15. $\frac{9}{10}y = -36$

16. $\frac{1}{2}m = \frac{6}{11}$

2-1

Practice (continued)

Form K

Solving One-Step Equations

Define a variable and write an equation for each situation. Then solve.

17. Bradley has a goal to work 28 hours each week at the pizza shop. So far he has worked 12 hours. How many more hours does he need to work to meet his goal?

18. Sheree is 4 times as old as Benjamin. If Sheree is 72 years old, how old is Benjamin?

Solve each equation. Check your answer.

19. $-8h = 26$

20. $-\frac{3}{5} = \frac{1}{10} + q$

21. $n + 3\frac{2}{3} = 5\frac{7}{9}$

22. $-9w = 6.3$

23. $5.8 = -4.5 + z$

24. $\frac{d}{5} = -\frac{3}{10}$

25. A youth club is taking a field trip to a community farm. 27 members attended the trip. The total cost for the club was $148.50.
   a. Write and solve an equation to determine the cost for each person.

   b. The farm brought in $1512.50 that day including what they received from the youth club. Write and solve an equation to find the number of people that visited the community farm that day.

2-1 Standardized Test Prep
Solving One-Step Equations

Multiple Choice

For Exercises 1–6, choose the correct letter.

1. What is the solution of $-3 = x + 5$?
   - **A.** -15
   - **B.** -8
   - **C.** 2
   - **D.** 8

2. What operation should you use to solve $-6x = -24$?
   - **F.** addition
   - **G.** subtraction
   - **H.** multiplication
   - **I.** division

3. Which of the following solutions is true for $\frac{x}{3} = \frac{1}{4}$?
   - **A.** $-2\frac{3}{4}$
   - **B.** $\frac{1}{12}$
   - **C.** $\frac{3}{4}$
   - **D.** $3\frac{1}{4}$

4. There are 37 more cats c than dogs d in an animal shelter. If there are 78 cats at the shelter, which equation represents the relationship between the number of cats and dogs?
   - **F.** $d + 37 = 78$
   - **G.** $d - 37 = 78$
   - **H.** $c + 37 = 78$
   - **I.** $c - 37 = 78$

5. Which property of equality should you use to solve $6x = 48$?
   - **A.** Addition Property of Equality
   - **B.** Subtraction Property of Equality
   - **C.** Multiplication Property of Equality
   - **D.** Division Property of Equality

6. Shelly completed 10 problems of her homework in study hall. This is $\frac{2}{7}$ of the total assignment. How many problems does she have left to complete?
   - **F.** 20
   - **G.** 25
   - **H.** 30
   - **I.** 35

Short Response

7. A high school marching band has 55 male members. It is determined that five-eighths of the band members are male.
   - **a.** What equation represents the total number of members in the band?
   - **b.** How many members are in the band?

2-1 Enrichment

Solving One-Step Equations

Equivalent equations are equations that have the same solution(s). For example, the equations $\frac{x}{3} = 6$ and $x - 6 = 12$ are equivalent because the solution of each is $x = 18$. Every equation has many equivalent equations.

There are four different forms of equations representing the four different operations mentioned in the lesson. If a and b represent constants, the different forms can be represented by the following equations:

1) $x + a = b$ 2) $ax = b$

3) $x - a = b$ 4) $\frac{x}{a} = b$

Determine which equations in the following exercises are equivalent. If they are equivalent, justify your answer. If not, explain.

1. $-2x = 14$ $x - 8 = -15$ $\frac{x}{7} = -1$ $-19 = x - 12$

2. $y - 8 = 12$ $\frac{y}{2} = 2$ $2y = 40$ $-22 = y - 42$

3. $-6n = -12$ $n + 8 = 6$ $-4 = n - 2$ $\frac{n}{2} = 1$

For each of the following equations, find three equivalent equations in the three other forms that are different from the original equation. For example, $x + 3 = 5$, $3x = 6$, and $\frac{x}{2} = 1$ are equivalent because $x = 2$ is the solution of each equation.

4. $x + 6 = -5$ **5.** $8x = -24$

6. $\frac{x}{3} = -9$ **7.** $14 = x - 18$

2-1

Reteaching

Solving One-Step Equations

You can use the properties of equality to solve equations. Subtraction is the inverse of addition.

Problem

What is the solution of $x + 5 = 33$?

In the equation, $x + 5 = 33$, 5 is added to the variable. To solve the equation, you need to isolate the variable, or get it alone on one side of the equal sign. Undo adding 5 by subtracting 5 from each side of the equation.

Drawing a diagram can help you write an equation to solve the problem.

Whole	
Part	Part

33	
X	5

Solve

$$x + 5 = 33$$

$$x + 5 - 5 = 33 - 5 \qquad \text{Undo adding 5 by subtracting 5.}$$

$$x = 28 \qquad \text{Simplify. This isolates } x.$$

Check

$$x + 5 = 33 \qquad \text{Check your solution in the original equation.}$$

$$28 + 5 \overset{?}{=} 33 \qquad \text{Substitute 28 for } x.$$

$$33 = 33 \checkmark$$

The solution to $x + 5 = 33$ is 28.

Division is the inverse of multiplication.

Problem

What is the solution of $\frac{x}{5} = 12$?

In the equation, $\frac{x}{5} = 12$, the variable is divided by 5. Undo

X				
12	12	12	12	12

dividing by 5 by multiplying by 5 on each side of the equation.

Solve

$$\frac{x}{5} = 12$$

$$\frac{x}{5} \cdot 5 = 12 \cdot 5 \qquad \text{Undo dividing by 5 by multiplying by 5.}$$

$$x = 60 \qquad \text{Simplify. This isolates } x.$$

The solution to $\frac{x}{5} = 12$ is 60.

2-1

Reteaching (continued)

Solving One-Step Equations

Exercises

Solve each equation using addition or subtraction. Check your answer.

1. $-3 = n + 9$ **2.** $f + 6 = -6$ **3.** $m + 12 = 22$

4. $r + 2 = 7$ **5.** $b + 1.1 = -11$ **6.** $t + 9 = 4$

Define a variable and write an equation for each situation. Then solve.

7. A student is taking a test. He has 37 questions left. If the test has 78 questions, how many questions has he finished?

8. A friend bought a bouquet of flowers. The bouquet had nine daisies and some roses. There were a total of 15 flowers in the bouquet. How many roses were in the bouquet?

Solve each equation using multiplication or division. Check your answer.

9. $\frac{z}{8} = 2$ **10.** $-26 = \frac{c}{13}$ **11.** $\frac{q}{11} = -6$

12. $-\frac{a}{3} = 18$ **13.** $-25 = \frac{g}{5}$ **14.** $20.4 = \frac{s}{2.5}$

15. A student has been typing for 22 minutes and has typed a total of 1496 words. Write and solve an equation to determine the average number of words she can type per minute.

2-2 ELL Support

Solving Two-Step Equations

Use the chart below to review vocabulary. These vocabulary words will help you complete this page.

Related Words	Explanations	Examples
solution suh loo shun	The value that makes an equation true A method for answering a problem	A solution to $x + 2 = 5$ is 3 because $3 + 2 = 5$.
solve sahlv	To work out a correct answer to a problem	She was able to solve the hardest problem on the test.
solving SAHL ving	Finding an answer to a problem	He spent an hour solving his homework problems.

Use the vocabulary above to fill in the blanks. The first one is done for you.

The teacher wants all her students to get the correct ___solution___ to the problem on the test.

1. The purpose of the test was to _____ ten problems.

2. _____ the easiest problem only took a minute.

Circle the correct answer.

3. What is the solution of the equation $2x - 35 = 15$?   10   15   20   25

4. Which answer solves the equation $5y + 25 = 50$?   5   10   25   50

Fill-in—the—blank

A package of flashcards tests addition, subtraction, multiplication, and division. There are 12 cards for each operation. Derek found a deck that has 46 cards. How many cards are missing from the deck?

Know

5. There are ☐ cards for each operation.

6. There are ☐ operations in a deck of flash cards.

7. How many cards did Derek find? ☐

Need

8. How many cards are in a full deck? ☐ × ☐ = ☐

Plan

9. To find the number of missing cards, you will need to _____

_____

2-2 Think About a Plan

Solving Two-Step Equations

Earth Science The temperature beneath Earth's surface increases by 10°C per kilometer. The surface temperature and the temperature at the bottom of a mine are shown. How many kilometers below Earth's surface is the bottom of the mine?

Surface: 18°C

Bottom of mine: 38°C

Understanding the Problem

1. What happens to the temperature as the distance below Earth's surface increases?

   _____

2. What do you need to determine?

   _____

3. What is the change in temperature from Earth's surface to the bottom of the mine?

   _____

Planning the Solution

4. Write an expression for how much the temperature increases x kilometers below the surface.

   _____

5. Write an equation that relates the change in temperature, from 18°C at Earth's surface to 38°C at the bottom of the mine, to the expression for how much the temperature increases x kilometers below the surface.

   _____

Getting an Answer

6. Solve the equation.

7. Is your answer reasonable? Explain.

   _____

   _____

2-2

Practice

Form G

Solving Two-Step Equations

Solve each equation. Check your answer.

1. $6 + 3b = -18$

2. $-3 + 5x = 12$

3. $7n + 12 = -23$

4. $\frac{t}{6} - 3 = 8$

5. $-12 = 8 + \frac{f}{2}$

6. $13 = 8 - 5d$

7. $\frac{k}{4} + 6 = -2$

8. $-22 = -8 + 7y$

9. $16 - 3p = 34$

10. $15 + \frac{q}{6} = -21$

11. $-19 + \frac{c}{3} = 8$

12. $-18 - 11r = 26$

13. $-9 = \frac{y}{-3} - 6$

14. $14 + \frac{m}{10} = 24$

Define a variable and write an equation for each situation. Then solve.

15. Chip earns a base salary of $500 per month as a salesman. In addition to the salary, he earns $90 per product that he sells. If his goal is to earn $5000 per month, how many products does he need to sell?

16. A pizza shop charges $9 for a large cheese pizza. Additional toppings cost $1.25 per topping. Heather paid $15.25 for her large pizza. How many toppings did she order?

2-2 Practice (continued) Form G

Solving Two-Step Equations

Solve each equation. Check your answer.

17. $\dfrac{z + 6}{3} = 8$

18. $\dfrac{n - 7}{2} = -11$

19. $\dfrac{j + 18}{-4} = 8$

20. $\dfrac{1}{3}a - 6 = -15$

21. $\dfrac{1}{4} = \dfrac{1}{4}h + 4$

22. $6.42 - 10d = 2.5$

23. The selling price of a television in a retail store is $66 less than 3 times the wholesale price. If the selling price of a television is $899, write and solve an equation to find the wholesale price of the television.

24. The fare for a taxicab is $5 per trip plus $0.50 per mile. The fare for the trip from the airport to the convention center was $11.50. Write and solve an equation to find how many miles the trip is from the airport to the convention center.

25. An online movie club offers a membership for $5 per month. Members can rent movies for $1.50 per rental. A member was billed $15.50 one month. Write and solve an equation to find how many movies the member rented.

26. Writing Describe, using words, how to solve the equation $6 - 4x = 18$. List any properties utilized in the solution.

27. a. Solve $-8 = \dfrac{x + 2}{4}$

b. Write the right side of the equation in part (a) as the sum of two fractions. Solve the equation.

c. Did you find the equation in part (a) or the rewritten equation easier to solve? Why?

Name _____ Class _____ Date _____

2-2 **Practice** Form K

Solving Two-Step Equations

Solve each equation. Check your answer.

1. $4x + 5 = 13$

2. $-8 + 3h = 1$

3. $2j - 13 = 25$

4. $\frac{n}{5} - 1 = 7$

5. $-5 = -8 + \frac{y}{10}$

6. $7 = -6m + 7$

7. $\frac{n}{-8} - 5 = -2$

8. $-14 = -6 + 4w$

9. $15 - 3t = -12$

10. $13 + \frac{a}{11} = 7$

Define a variable and write an equation for each situation. Then solve.

11. A fair charges $7.25 for admission and $5.50 for a ride pass. Ten friends visited the fair. Not all of the friends purchased ride passes. If their total cost was $105.50, how many friends purchased ride passes?

12. A cafeteria sells entrées and additional items. An entrée costs $4.75, and each additional item costs $1.25. A customer pays $9.75 for one entree and some additional items. How many additional items were ordered?

2-2 Practice (continued) Form K
Solving Two-Step Equations

Solve each equation. Check your answer.

13. $\dfrac{f + 4}{2} = 5$

14. $\dfrac{p - 6}{3} = -15$

15. $\dfrac{c + 5}{-6} = -4$

16. $\frac{1}{4}z + 9 = -1$

17. $\frac{1}{2} = \frac{1}{2}t + 3$

18. $4.52 - 5h = 2.8$

19. Jasmine is 23 years old. Jasmine is 3 years less than half of George's age. Write and solve an equation to find George's age.

20. An appliance repair person charges $55 per trip plus $15 per hour for her labor. The cost of fixing a stove was $92.50. Write and solve an equation to find how many hours it took to repair the stove.

21. Shelly has a cell phone plan that costs $9.99 per month plus $0.05 per minute. Her total bill for the month is $25.59. Write and solve an equation to find how many minutes she used for the month.

22. **Writing** Describe using words how to solve the equation $3 - 5n = -22$. Describe the properties utilized in the solution.

2-2

Standardized Test Prep

Solving Two-Step Equations

Gridded Response

Solve each exercise and enter your answer on the grid provided.

1. What is the solution of $-28 = 22 - 5x$?

2. What is the solution of $\frac{m}{4} - 3 = 7$?

3. The amount of money that Pamela p has and Julie j has are related by the equation $3p + 5 = j$. If Julie has \$83, how much money does Pamela have?

4. An ice cream sundae costs \$1.75 plus an additional \$0.35 for each topping. If the total cost is \$2.80, how many toppings did the sundae have?

5. The cost of a gallon of gasoline g is \$3.25 less than 2 times the cost of a gallon of diesel d. If a gallon of gasoline costs \$3.95, what is the cost of a gallon of diesel?

1. 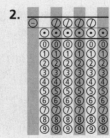   2. 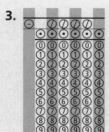   3. 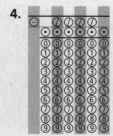   4. 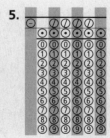   5.

2-2

Enrichment

Solving Two-Step Equations

Equations are used in geometry. One example is the relationship between the angles that are formed by intersecting lines. The measures of the pairs of opposite angles are equal. The measures of two adjacent angles add up to 180°.

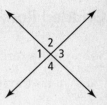

Use the drawing shown to answer the following questions.

1. $m\angle 1 = 30$ and $m\angle 2 = 4x$. What is the value of x?

2. $m\angle 3 = 5x$ and $m\angle 4 = 75$. What is the value of x?

3. $m\angle 4 = 45$ and $m\angle 2 = 9x$. What is the value of x?

The formula for the perimeter of a rectangle is $P = 2l + 2w$, where l is the length and w is the width of the rectangle.

4. The width of a rectangle is 12 ft. The perimeter of the rectangle is 42 ft. What is the length of the rectangle?

5. The perimeter of a rectangle is 158.5 cm. The length of the rectangle is 42.5 cm. What is the width of the rectangle?

Another geometric application for 2-step equations involves the measures of the interior angles of a polygon. Regardless of the number of sides, n, a polygon has, the sum of the measures of the interior angles is $180n - 360$ degrees.

For example, the sum of the measures of the angles of a rectangle is $180(4) - 360 = 360°$.

The sum of the measures of the interior angles of various polygons are given. Set up an equation and solve to find the number of sides of each polygon.

6. 1080°   **7.** 1440°   **8.** 2340°

9. 180°   **10.** 3600°   **11.** 540°

2-2 Reteaching

Solving Two-Step Equations

Properties of equality and inverse operations can be used to solve equations that involve more than one step to solve. To solve a two-step equation, identify the operations and undo them using inverse operations. Undo the operations in the reverse order of the order of operations.

Problem

What is the solution of $5x - 8 = 32$?

$5x - 8 + 8 = 32 + 8$	To get the variable term alone on the left side, add 8 to each side.
$5x = 40$	Simplify.
$\dfrac{5x}{5} = \dfrac{40}{5}$	Divide each side by 5 since x is being multiplied by 5 on the left side. This isolates x.
$x = 8$	Simplify.
Check $5x - 8 = 32$	Check your solution in the original equation.
$5(8) - 8 = 32$	Substitute 8 for x.
$32 = 32 \checkmark$	Simplify.

To solve $-16 = \frac{x}{3} + 5$, you can use subtraction first to undo the addition, and then use multiplication to undo the division.

Problem

What is the solution of $-16 = \frac{x}{3} + 5$?

$-16 - 5 = \frac{x}{3} + 5 - 5$	To get the variable term alone on the right, subtract 5 from each side.
$-21 = \frac{x}{3}$	Simplify.
$3(-21) = 3\left(\frac{x}{3}\right)$	Since x is being divided by 3, multiply each side by 3 to undo the division. This isolates x.
$-63 = x$	Simplify.

2-2 **Reteaching** (continued)

Solving Two-Step Equations

Solve each equation. Check your answer.

1. $4f - 8 = 20$

2. $25 - 6b = 55$

3. $-z + 7 = -8$

4. $\frac{w}{-9} + 7 = 10$

5. $25 = 8 + \frac{n}{2}$

6. $\frac{y - 8}{3} = -7$

Solve each equation. Justify each step.

7. $6d - 5 = 31$

8. $\frac{p - 7}{-2} = 5$

Define a variable and write an equation for each situation. Then solve.

9. Ray's birthday is 8 more than four times the number of days away from today than Jane's birthday. If Ray's birthday is 24 days from today, how many days until Jane's birthday?

10. Jerud weighs 15 pounds less than twice Kate's weight. How much does Kate weigh if Jerud weighs 205 pounds?

11. A phone company charges a flat fee of $17 per month, which includes free local calling plus $0.08 per minute for long distance calls. The Taylor's phone bill for the month is $31.80. How many minutes of long distance calling did they use during the month?

12. A delivery company charges a flat rate of $3 for a large envelope plus an additional $0.25 per ounce for every ounce over a pound the package weighs. The postage for the package is $5.50. How much does the package weigh? (Hint: remember the first pound is included in the $3.)

2-3 ELL Support

Solving Multi-Step Equations

Problem

What is the solution of the multi-step equation $3x + 7 + 6x = 34$**? Justify your steps. Then check your solution.**

$3x + 7 + 6x = 34$	Write the original equation.
$3x + 6x + 7 = 34$	Commutative Property of Addition
$9x + 7 = 34$	Combine like terms.
$9x + \boxed{7 - 7} = 34 - 7$	Subtract 7 from each side. Subtraction Property of Equality
$9x = 27$	Simplify.
$\frac{9x}{9} = \frac{27}{9}$	Divide each side by 9. Division Property of Equality
$x = 3$	Simplify.

Check

$3x + 7 + 6x = 34$	Copy the original equation.
$3(3) + 7 + 6(3) = 34$	Substitute 3 for x.
$9 + 7 + 18 = 34$	Simplify.
$34 = 34$ ✓	

Exercise

What is the solution to the multi-step equation $4d - 2 + 3d = 61$**? Justify your steps. Then check your solution.**

$4d - 2 + 3d = 61$	_____
$4d + 3d - 2 = 61$	_____
$7d - 2 = 61$	_____
$7d - 2 + 2 = 61 + 2$	_____
$7d = 63$	_____
$\frac{7d}{7} = \frac{63}{7}$	_____
$d = 9$	_____

Check

$4d - 2 + 3d = 61$	Copy the original equation.
$4(9) - 2 + 3(9) = 61$	Substitute ____ for d.
$\boxed{} - 2 + \boxed{} = 61$	Simplify.
$\boxed{} = 61$ ____	

2-3   Think About a Plan

Solving Multi-Step Equations

Online Video Games Angie and Kenny play online video games. Angie buys 1 software package and 3 months of game play. Kenny buys 1 software package and 2 months of game play. Each software package costs $20. If their total cost is $115, what is the cost of one month of game play?

Know

1. What values are you given?

_____

_____

Need

2. What do you need to find?

_____

Plan

3. What equation can you use to solve the problem?

_____

4. Solve the equation. Show your work and justify each step.

_____

_____

_____

_____

_____

5. Check your answer.

_____

_____

6. Is your answer reasonable? Explain.

_____

_____

2-3 Practice   Form G

Solving Multi-Step Equations

Solve each equation. Check your answer.

1. $19 - h - h = -13$

2. $14 + 6a - 8 = 18$

3. $25 = 7 + 3k - 12$

4. $5n - 16 - 8n = -10$

5. $-34 = v + 42 - 5v$

6. $x - 1 + 5x = 23$

7. $42j + 18 - 19j = -28$

8. $-49 = 6c - 13 - 4c$

9. $-28 + 15 - 22z = 31$

Write an equation to model each situation. Then solve the equation.

10. General admission tickets to the fair cost $3.50 per person. Ride passes cost an additional $5.50 per person. Parking costs $6 for the family. The total costs for ride passes and parking was $51. How many people in the family attended the fair?

11. Five times a number decreased by 18 minus 4 times the same number is −36. What is the number?

Solve each equation. Check your answer.

12. $6(3m + 5) = 66$

13. $3(4y - 8) = 12$

14. $-5(x - 3) = -25$

15. $42 = 3(2 - 3h)$

16. $-10 = 5(2w - 4)$

17. $(3p - 4) = 31$

18. $-3 = -3(2t - 1)$

19. $x - 2(x + 10) = 12$

20. $-15 = 5(3q - 10) - 5q$

21. Angela ate at the same restaurant four times. Each time she ordered a salad and left a $5 tip. She spent a total of $54. Write and solve an equation to find the cost of each salad.

2-3

Practice (continued)

Form G

Solving Multi-Step Equations

Solve each equation. Choose the method you prefer to use. Check your answer.

22. $\frac{a}{7} + \frac{5}{7} = \frac{2}{7}$

23. $6v - \frac{5}{8} = \frac{7}{8}$

24. $\frac{j}{6} - 9 = \frac{5}{6}$

25. $\frac{x}{3} - \frac{1}{2} = \frac{3}{4}$

26. $\frac{g}{5} + \frac{5}{6} = 6$

27. $\frac{b}{9} - \frac{1}{2} = \frac{5}{18}$

28. $0.52y + 2.5 = 5.1$

29. $4n + 0.24 = 15.76$

30. $2.45 - 3.1t = 21.05$

31. $-4.2 = 9.1x + 23.1$

32. $11.3 - 7.2f = -3.82$

33. $14.2 = -6.8 + 4.2d$

34. Reasoning Suppose you want to solve $-5 = 6x + 3 + 7x$. What would you do as your first step? Explain.

35. Writing Describe two different ways to solve $-10 = \frac{1}{4}(8y - 12)$.

Solve each equation. Round to the nearest hundredth if necessary.

36. $5 + \frac{2a}{-3} = \frac{5}{11}$

37. $\frac{3}{5}(p - 3) = -4$

38. $11m - (6m - 5) = 25$

39. The sum of three integers is 228. The second integer is 1 more than the first, and the third integer is 2 more than the first. Write an equation to determine the integers. Solve your equation. Show your work.

40. Can you solve the equation $\frac{2}{3}(4x - 5) = 8$ by using the Division Property of Equality? Explain.

2-3

Practice

Form K

Solving Multi-Step Equations

Solve each equation. Check your answer.

1. $20 + g + g = 14$

2. $7 + 4x - 9 = -6$

3. $-12 = -5 - 6n + 11$

4. $t + 10 - 4t = -11$

5. $8 = 8p + 13 - 3p$

6. $4y - 16 + 8y = -4$

Write an equation to model each situation. Then solve the equation.

7. A plumber finished three jobs on Tuesday. The first two only cost the owner the $45 trip fee because they took very little time to complete. For the third job, the plumber charged the trip fee plus 6 times his hourly rate. If the plumber received a total of $303 for the day, what is the hourly rate?

8. Three times a number plus 12 minus 5 times the same number is 22. What is the number?

Solve each equation. Check your answer.

9. $4(-2d - 3) = 12$

10. $5(5t - 2) = -35$

11. $-2(a + 6) = -22$

12. $60 = 6(6 - 2n)$

13. $-14 = -4(9x - 1)$

14. $-(5z + 12) = 18$

2-3 Practice (continued) Form K

Solving Multi-Step Equations

15. Eli took the fleet of 8 vans for oil changes. All of the vans needed windshield wipers which cost $24 per van. The total bill was $432. Write an equation to find out what each oil change cost. Solve the equation.

Solve each equation. Choose the method you prefer. Check your answer.

16. $\frac{m}{3} + \frac{1}{3} = \frac{2}{3}$

17. $5r - \frac{1}{5} = \frac{4}{5}$

18. $\frac{w}{9} - 6 = \frac{7}{9}$

19. $1.75t - 4.5 = 7.75$

20. $6z + 0.36 = 24.72$

21. $7.85 - 2.15c = 20.75$

22. Writing Describe the first step you would take in solving $12 = 7 - 3x + 5x$. Explain.

23. Writing Describe how you would solve $-8 = \frac{1}{9}(-9t + 27)$.

Solve each equation. Round to the nearest hundredth if necessary.

24. $11 + \frac{4x}{-5} = \frac{2}{3}$

25. $\frac{5}{7}(k + 5) = -7$

26. Reasoning Can you solve the equation $\frac{3}{4}(6x + 9) = 14$ by using the Division Property of Equality? Explain.

2-3

Standardized Test Prep

Solving Multi-Step Equations

Multiple Choice

For Exercises 1–5, choose the correct letter.

1. What is the solution of $-17 = -2n + 13 - 8n$?

   A. -3 **B.** $-\frac{2}{3}$ **C.** 3   **D.** 5

2. What is the solution of $-4(-3m - 2) = 32$?

   F. -2 **G.** 2   **H.** 4   **I.** 6

3. What is the solution of $\frac{x}{3} + \frac{3}{5} = -\frac{1}{15}$?

   A. -2 **B.** $\frac{8}{5}$ **C.** 2   **D.** $\frac{16}{3}$

4. When the sum of a number and 7 is multiplied by 4, the result is 16. What is the original number?

   F. -12 **G.** -3 **H.** 3   **I.** 11

5. A merchant is selling wind chimes from a booth at a flea market. He rents his space for $125 per day. The profit from each wind chime sold is $12. His goal is to make $3500 in a five day work week. Which equation represents how many chimes he needs to sell in a week to meet his goal?

   A. $12c - 625 = 3500$

   B. $5(12c) - 125 = 3500$

   C. $5(12c + 125) = 3500$

   D. $5(12c - 125) = 3500$

Short Response

6. Four friends are planning to play 18 holes of golf. Two of them need to rent clubs at $5 per set. Cart rental is $10. The total cost of the golf outing, including green fees, is $92.

   a. Write an equation to represent the total cost of the golf outing per player.

   b. How much did the friends pay in green fees?

2-3

Enrichment

Solving Multi-Step Equations

Consecutive integers are simply integers that follow each other in order.
For example, 1, 2, and 3, are consecutive integers. Algebraically, these consecutive
integers can be represented as follows:

$$1 \quad \rightarrow \quad N$$

$$2 \quad \rightarrow \quad N + 1$$

$$3 \quad \rightarrow \quad N + 2$$

Therefore, the sum of three consecutive integers is written as

$$N + (N + 1) + (N + 2)$$

So, consecutive even integers would be represented by N, $N + 2$, and $N + 4$,
where N must be an even integer. Consecutive odd integers would also be
represented by N, $N + 2$, and $N + 4$, where N must be an odd integer.

1. Find three consecutive even integers whose sum is 48.

2. Find three consecutive odd integers whose sum is 141.

3. Find three consecutive even integers whose sum is −240.

4. Find three consecutive odd integers whose sum is −465.

5. Find three consecutive integers whose sum is 300.

6. Find three consecutive integers whose sum of the first and the third is −88.

7. Find three consecutive integers for which 3 times the sum of the first and the
   third integers is −342.

8. Find three consecutive even integers for which −4 times the sum of the first
   and the third integers is 192.

Name _____ Class _____ Date _____

2-3 Reteaching
Solving Multi-Step Equations

To solve multi-step equations, use properties of equality, inverse operations, the Distributive Property, and properties of real numbers to isolate the variable. Like terms on either side of the equation should be combined first.

Problem

a) What is the solution of $-3y + 8 + 13y = -52$?

$-3y + 13y + 8 = -52$	Group the terms with y together so that the like terms are grouped together.
$10y + 8 = -52$	Add the coefficients to combine like terms.
$10y + 8 - 8 = -52 - 8$	To get the variable term by itself on the left side, subtract 8 from each side.
$10y = -60$	Simplify.
$\frac{10y}{10} = \frac{-60}{10}$	Divide each side by 10 since y is being multiplied by 10 on the left side. This isolates y.
$y = -6$	Simplify.

b) What is the solution of $-2(3n - 4) = -10$?

$-6n + 8 = -10$	Distribute the -2 into the parentheses by multiplying each term inside by -2.
$-6n + 8 - 8 = -10 - 8$	To get the variable term by itself on the left side, subtract 8 from each side.
$-6n = -18$	Simplify.
$\frac{-6n}{-6} = \frac{-18}{-6}$	Divide each side by -6 since n is being multiplied by -6 on the left side. This isolates n.
$n = 3$	Simplify.

Solve each equation. Check your answer.

1. $4 - 6h - 8h = 60$

2. $-32 = -7n - 12 + 3n$

3. $14 + 12 = -15x + 2x$

4. $8(-3d + 2) = 88$

5. $-22 = -(x - 4)$

6. $35 = -5(2k + 5)$

7. $3m + 6 - 2m = -22$

8. $4(3r + 2) - 3r = -10$

9. $-18 = 15 - 3(6t + 5)$

10. $-5 + 2(10b - 2) = 31$

11. $7 = 5x + 3(x - 2) + 5$

12. $-18 = 3(-z + 6) + 2z$

13. Reasoning Solve the equation $14 = 7(2x - 4)$ using two different methods. Show your work. Which method do you prefer? Explain.

2-3 Reteaching (continued)
Solving Multi-Step Equations

Equations with fractions can be solved by using a common denominator or by eliminating the fractions altogether.

Problem

What is the solution of $\frac{x}{4} - \frac{2}{3} = \frac{7}{12}$?

Method 1

Get a common denominator first.

$$\frac{3}{3}\left(\frac{x}{4}\right) - \frac{4}{4}\left(\frac{2}{3}\right) = \frac{7}{12}$$
$$\frac{3x}{12} - \frac{8}{12} = \frac{7}{12}$$
$$\frac{3x}{12} = \frac{15}{12}$$
$$\frac{3x}{12} \cdot \frac{12}{3} = \frac{15}{12} \cdot \frac{12}{3}$$
$$x = 5$$

Method 2

Multiply by the common denominator first.

$$12\left(\frac{x}{4} - \frac{2}{3}\right) = 12\left(\frac{7}{12}\right)$$
$${}^3\cancel{12}\left(\frac{x}{\cancel{4}}\right) - {}^4\cancel{12}\left(\frac{2}{\cancel{3}}\right) = \cancel{12}\left(\frac{7}{\cancel{12}}\right)$$
$$3x - 8 = 7$$
$$3x = 15$$
$$x = 5$$

Decimals can be cleared from the equation by multiplying by a power of ten with the same number of zeros as the number of digits to the right of the decimal. For instance, if the greatest number of digits after the decimal is 3, like 4.586, you multiply by 1000.

Problem

What is the solution of $2.8x - 4.25 = 5.55$?

$100(2.8x - 4.25 = 5.55)$ — Multiply by 100 because the most number of digits after the decimal is two.

$280x - 425 = 555$ — Simplify by moving the decimal point to the right 2 places in each term.

$280x = 980$ — Add 425 to each side to get the term with the variable by itself on the left side.

$x = 3.5$ — Divide each side by 280 to isolate the variable.

Solve each equation. Check your answer.

14. $\frac{x}{16} - \frac{1}{2} = \frac{3}{8}$ **15.** $\frac{2a}{3} + \frac{8}{9} = 4$ **16.** $\frac{3n}{7} - 1 = \frac{1}{8}$

17. $-1.68j + 1.24 = 13$ **18.** $4.6 = 3.5w - 6.6$ **19.** $5.23y + 3.02 = -2.21$

2-4

ELL Support

Solving Equations with Variables on Both Sides

Choose the word from the list that best matches each sentence.

> equation   identity   solution   variable

1. A placeholder for an unknown number. _____

2. A value of the variable that makes the equation true. _____

3. A mathematical sentence that states two quantities are equal. _____

4. A mathematical sentence that is true for every value. _____

5. In the equation $x + 12 = 34$, x is a _____.

6. A mathematical sentence that uses an equal sign, $=$, is called an _____.

7. An _____ that is true for every value is called an _____.

8. $3x = x + 2x$ is an _____ because it is true for all values of x.

9. A symbol, usually a letter, that represents one or more numbers is called a _____.

10. In the equation $y - 15 = 34$, the number 49 is the _____.

Circle all the variables in the equation.

11. $9w - 7 = 3w + 23$

12. $(5 - 6t) = \frac{t}{5} + 7$

Multiple Choice

13. Which of the following is an equation?

A) $3x - 6$ B) $5m$ C) $7w + 4 = 25$ D) $48 + 27y$

2-4 Think About a Plan

Solving Equations With Variables on Both Sides

Skiing A skier is trying to decide whether or not to buy a season ski pass. A daily pass costs $67. A season ski pass costs $350. The skier would have to rent skis with either pass for $25 per day. How many days would the skier have to go skiing in order to make the season pass less expensive than daily passes?

Understanding the Problem

1. What do you know about the costs associated with buying a daily pass?

   _____

2. What do you know about the costs associated with buying a season pass?

   _____

Planning the Solution

3. Write an expression using words to represent the cost of a daily pass. Write the algebraic expression.

   _____

   _____

4. Write an expression using words to represent the cost of a season pass. Write the algebraic expression.

   _____

   _____

5. How can you compare the cost of a daily pass with the cost of a season pass algebraically? What is the equation?

   _____

   _____

Getting an Answer

6. Solve the equation you wrote in Step 5. Show your work.

   _____

   _____

7. Explain what this solution means.

   _____

2-4 Practice

Form G

Solving Equations With Variables on Both Sides

Solve each equation. Check your answer.

1. $3n + 2 = -2n - 8$

2. $8b - 7 = 7b - 2$

3. $-12 + 5k = 15 - 4k$

4. $-q - 11 = 2q + 4$

5. $4t + 9 = -8t - 13$

6. $22p + 11 = 4p - 7$

7. $17 - 9y = -3 + 16y$

8. $15m + 22 = -7m + 18$

9. $3x + 7 = 14 + 3x$

Write and solve an equation for each situation. Check your solution.

10. Shirley is going to have the exterior of her home painted. Tim's Painting charges $250 plus $14 per hour. Colorful Paints charges $22 per hour. How many hours would the job need to take for Tim's Painting to be the better deal?

11. Tracey is looking at two different travel agencies to plan her vacation. ABC Travel offers a plane ticket for $295 and a rental car for $39 per day. M & N Travel offers a plane ticket for $350 and a rental car for $33 per day. What is the minimum number of days that Shirley's vacation should be for M & N Travel to have the better deal?

Solve each equation. Check your answer.

12. $7(h + 3) = 6(h - 3)$

13. $-(5a + 6) = 2(3a + 8)$

14. $-2(2f - 4) = -4(-f + 2)$

15. $3w - 6 + 2w = -2 + w$

16. $-8x - (3x + 6) = 4 - x$

17. $14 + 3n = 8n - 3(n - 4)$

Determine whether each equation is an *identity* or whether it has *no solution*.

18. $4(3m + 4) = 2(6m + 8)$

19. $5x + 2x - 3 = -3x + 10x$

20. $-(3z + 4) = 6z - 3(3z + 2)$

21. $-2(j - 3) = -2j + 6$

2-4 **Practice** (continued)   Form G

Solving Equations With Variables on Both Sides

Solve each equation. If the equation is an identity, write _identity_. If it has no solution, write _no solution_.

22. $6.8 - 4.2b = 5.6b - 3$

23. $\frac{1}{3} + \frac{2}{3}m = \frac{2}{3}m - \frac{2}{3}$

24. $-2(5.25 + 6.2x) = 4(-3.1x + 2.68)$

25. $\frac{1}{2}r + 6 = 3 - 2r$

26. $0.5t + 0.25(t + 16) = 4 + 0.75t$

27. $2.5(2z + 5) = 5(z + 2.5)$

28. $-6(-p + 8) = -6p + 12$

29. $\frac{3}{8}f + \frac{1}{2} = 6(\frac{1}{16}f - 3)$

30. Three times the sum of a number and 4 is 8 less than one-half the number. Write and solve an equation to find the number.

31. A square and a rectangle have the same perimeters. The length of a side of the square is $4x - 1$. The length of the rectangle is $2x + 1$ and the width is $x + 2$. Write and solve an equation to find x.

32. A movie club charges a one-time membership fee of $25 which allows members to purchase movies for $7 each. Another club does not charge a membership fee and sells movies for $12 each. How many movies must a member purchase for the cost of the two clubs to be equal?

33. Writing Describe the difference between an equation that is defined as an identity and an equation that has no solution. Provide an example of each and explain why each example is an identity or has no solution.

2-4 Practice

Form K

Solving Equations With Variables on Both Sides

Solve each equation. Check your answer.

1. $4y + 15 = 6y - 11$

2. $5p + 6 = -4p - 8$

3. $13k + 5 = k - 7$

4. $6q - 1 = -q + 20$

5. $25h + 40 = -15h - 80$

6. $-2m + 13 = 2m - 3$

Write and solve an equation for each situation. Check your solution.

7. Suzanne is going to rent a car while she is out of town. One car rental company offers a flat rate of $35 per day plus $0.10 per mile. Another car rental company offers the same car for $25 per day plus $0.25 per mile. She will need the car for 5 days. How many miles would she need to drive for the first rental company to be the better deal?

8. Jeremy is looking at two different lawncare companies to weed and mulch his flower beds. Greenscape Lawncare offers to charge $100 for the mulch plus $12 per hr for the labor. D & J Landscape offers to charge $23 per hr for the job including the mulch. What is the minimum number of hours the job could be for D & J Landscape to have the better deal?

Solve each equation. Check your answer.

9. $4(h + 2) = 3(h - 2)$

10. $-(3b - 15) = 6(2b + 5)$

11. $5x + 7 + 3x = -8 + 3x$

12. $18 - 6a = 4a - 4(a + 3)$

2-4 Practice (continued)   Form K

Solving Equations With Variables on Both Sides

Solve each equation. If the equation is an identity, write _identity_. If it has no solution, write _no solution_.

13. $6(4z + 2) = 3(8z + 4)$

14. $-8t - 3t + 2 = -5t - 6t$

15. $-(8m + 4) = 4m - 2(6m + 2)$

16. $-5(x + 7) = -5x + 35$

17. $5.5 - 3b = 2b - 6.25$

18. $\frac{3}{4} + \frac{1}{4}m = \frac{3}{4}m - \frac{1}{4}$

19. $-5(5.25 + 3.1x) = -6.2(2.5x + 1.9)$

20. $\frac{2}{3}h - 9 = 6 - \frac{2}{3}h$

21. $0.2f + 0.6(f + 20) = -8 + 0.4f$

22. $-2(-w + 11) = -13 + 2w - 9$

23. Six times the sum of a number and 3 is 12 less than 12 times the number. Write and solve an equation to find the number.

24. A triangle with equal sides and a square have the same perimeters. The length of a side of the triangle is $2x + 2$. The length of a side of the square is $x + 8$. Write and solve an equation to find x.

25. Open-Ended Give one example of an equation with variables on both sides that is an identity and one equation with variables on both sides that has no solution. Justify your examples by solving the equations.

2-4 Standardized Test Prep

Solving Equations With Variables on Both Sides

Multiple Choice

For Exercises 1–5, choose the correct letter.

1. What is the solution of $-8x - 5 + 3x = 7 + 4x - 9$?

   A. -3 **B.** $-\frac{1}{3}$ **C.** $\frac{1}{3}$ **D.** 3

2. What is the solution of $-(-5 - 6x) = 4(5x + 3)$?

   F. -2 **G.** $-\frac{1}{2}$ **H.** $\frac{1}{2}$ **I.** 2

3. What is the solution of $2n - 3(4n + 5) = -6(n - 3) - 1$?

   A. -8 **B.** -6 **C.** $-\frac{1}{2}$ **D.** 4

4. Negative one times the sum of twice a number and 3 is equal to two times the difference of -4 times the number and 3. What is the number?

   F. -4 **G.** -2 **H.** $-\frac{1}{2}$ **I.** 2

5. Jacob is saving for a new bicycle which costs $175. He has already saved $35. His goal is to have enough money saved in six weeks to pay for the bicycle. Which equation represents how much money he needs to save each week to meet his goal?

   A. $35 + 6d = 175$

   B. $35 + 12d = 175$

   C. $6(35 + 2d) = 175$

   D. $2(35 + 6d) = 175$

Short Response

6. Admission for a water park is $17.50 per day. A season pass costs $125. A locker rental costs $3.50 per day.

   a. What is an equation that represents the relationship between the cost of a daily pass and the cost of a season pass?

   b. How many days would you have to go to the water park for the season pass to save you money?

2-4 | Enrichment

Solving Equations With Variables on Both Sides

The circumference and area of a circle are determined by the formulas $C = 2\pi r$ and $A = \pi r^2$. An increase of 1 unit in the radius causes predictable increases in the circumference and area.

Start with a circle of radius 1 unit. Then $C = 2\pi$ units and $A = \pi$ square units. Increasing the radius by 1 unit, meaning $r = 2$, leads to $C = 4\pi$ units and $A = 4\pi$ square units. Increasing the radius by 1 unit again, meaning $r = 3$, leads to $C = 6\pi$ and $A = 9\pi$. You may notice a pattern emerging.

Even if the radius is not known, knowing by how much the radius changes makes it possible to compare the circumference and area of the new circle to the circumference and area of the old circle.

For a circle with radius x, $C = 2\pi x$ and $A = \pi x^2$.
If the radius is increased by 1 unit to $x + 1$, $C = 2\pi(x + 1)$ or $2\pi x + 2\pi$, and $A = \pi(x + 1)^2$ or $\pi(x^2 + 2x + 1)$.

1. The circumference of a circle is 8π cm. The radius is increased, and the circumference of the new circle is 16π cm. By how much was the radius of the original circle increased?

2. One circle has a radius 1 unit greater than another circle. The area of the larger circle is 9π square units greater than the area of the smaller circle. What are the radius and area of each circle?

3. If the radius of a circle is increased by 1 unit, the area of the circle is increased by 16π square units. What is the radius of the original circle?

4. By how many units must the radius of a circle be increased to increase its circumference by 22π units?

5. The circumference of a circle is 4 times the circumference of a circle with a radius 1 unit less. What is the radius of each circle?

2-4 Reteaching

Solving Equations With Variables on Both Sides

To solve equations with variables on both sides, you can use the properties of equality and inverse operations to write a series of simpler equivalent equations.

Problem

What is the solution of $2m - 4 + 5m = 13 - 6m - 4$?

$7m - 4 = -6m + 9$	Add the terms with variables together on the left side and the constants on the right side to combine like terms.
$7m - 4 + 6m = -6m + 9 + 6m$	To move the variables to the left side, add $6m$ to each side.
$13m - 4 = 9$	Simplify.
$13m - 4 + 4 = 9 + 4$	To get the variable term alone on the left, add 4 to each side.
$13m = 13$	Simplify.
$\frac{13m}{13} = \frac{13}{13}$	Divide each side by 13 since x is being multiplied by 13 on the left side. This isolates x.
$m = 1$	Simplify.

Problem

What is the solution of $3(5x - 2) = -3(x + 6)$?

$15x - 6 = -3x - 18$	Distribute 3 on the left side and -3 on the right side into the parentheses by multiplying them by each term inside.
$15x - 6 + 6 = -3x - 18 + 6$	To move all of the terms without a variable to the right side, add 6 to each side.
$15x = -3x - 12$	Simplify.
$15x + 3x = -3x - 12 + 3x$	To get the variable terms to the left side, add $3x$ to each side.
$18x = -12$	Simplify.
$\frac{18x}{18} = -\frac{12}{18}$	Divide each side by 18 since x is being multiplied by 18 on the left side. This isolates x.
$x = -\frac{2}{3}$	Simplify and reduce the fraction.

Solve each equation. Check your answer.

1. $-5x + 9 = -3x + 1$ **2.** $14 + 7n = 14n + 28$ **3.** $22(g - 1) = 2g + 8$

4. $-d + 12 - 3d = 5d - 6$ **5.** $4(m - 2) = -2(3m + 3)$ **6.** $-(4y - 8) = 2(y + 4)$

7. $5a - 2(4a + 5) = 7a$ **8.** $11w + 2(3w - 1) = 15w$ **9.** $4(3 - 5p) = -5(3p + 3)$

2-4 Reteaching (continued)

Solving Equations With Variables on Both Sides

An equation that is true for every value of the variable for which the equation is defined is an identity. For example, $x - 5 = x - 5$ is an identity because the equation is true for any value of x. An equation has no solution if there is no value of the variable that makes the equation true. The equation $x + 6 = x + 3$ has no solution.

Problem

What is the solution of each equation?

a) $3(4x - 2) = -2(-6x + 3)$

$12x - 6 = 12x - 6$	Distribute 3 on the left side and -2 on the right side into the parentheses by multiplying them by each term inside.
$12x - 6 - 12x = 12x - 6 - 12x$	To get the variable terms to the left side, subtract $12x$ from each side.
$-6 = -6$	Simplify.

Because $-6 = -6$ is always true, there are infinitely many solutions of the original equation. The equation is an identity.

b) $2n + 4(n - 2) = 8 + 6n$

$2n + 4n - 8 = 8 + 6n$	Distribute 4 into the parentheses by multiplying it by each term inside.
$6n - 8 = 8 + 6n$	Add the variable terms on the left side to combine like terms.
$6n - 8 - 6n = 8 + 6n - 6n$	To get the variable terms to the left side, subtract $6n$ from each side.
$-8 = 8$	Simplify.

Since $-8 \neq 8$, the equation has no solution.

Determine whether each equation is an _identity_ or whether it has _no solution_.

10. $-3(2x + 1) = 2(-3x - 1)$ **11.** $4(-3x + 4) = -2(6x - 8)$ **12.** $3n + 3(-n + 3) = 3$

Solve each equation. If the equation is an identity, write _identity_. If it has no solution, write _no solution_.

13. $-(4n + 2) = -2(2n - 1)$ **14.** $2(-d + 4) = 2d + 8$ **15.** $-k - 18 = -5 - k - 13$

16. Open-Ended Write three equations with variables on both sides of the equal sign with one having no solution, one having exactly one solution, and one being an identity.

2-5

ELL Support

Literal Equations and Formulas

There are two sets of cards below that show how to solve $12c + 2d = 48g$ for d.
The set on the left explains the thinking. The set on the right shows the steps.
Write the thinking and the steps in the correct order.

Think Cards

Subtract 12c from each side.

Divide each side by 2.

Copy the problem.

Simplify.

Divide each term by 2 to simplify.

Write Cards

$2d = 48g - 12c$

$12c + 2d - 12c = 48g - 12c$

$\dfrac{2d}{2} = \dfrac{48g - 12c}{2}$

$d = 24g - 6c$

$12c + 2d = 48g$

Think	**Write**
First,	Step 1
Second,	Step 2
Next,	Step 3
Then,	Step 4
Finally,	Step 5

2-5

Think About a Plan

Literal Equations and Formulas

Density The density of an object is calculated using the formula $D = \frac{m}{V}$, where m is the object's mass and V is its volume. Gold has a density of 19.3 g/cm^3. What is the volume of an amount of gold that has a mass of 96.5 g?

KNOW

1. What is the formula you are given for the density of an object?

_____

2. What values are you given in the problem?

_____

_____

NEED

3. What measurement are you asked to determine?

_____

4. Solve $D = \frac{m}{V}$ for the variable V. Show your work.

_____

_____

_____

PLAN

5. Write your new formula. Substitute the values you are given into the formula.

_____

6. What is the volume of 96.5 g of gold?

_____

7. In what units is your answer? Do these units make sense? Explain.

_____

_____

2-5 Practice

Form G

Literal Equations and Formulas

Solve each equation for *m*. Then find the value of *m* for each value of *n*.

1. $m + 3n = 7$; $n = -2, 0, 1$

2. $3m - 9n = 24$; $n = -1, 1, 3$

3. $-5n = 4m + 8$; $n = -1, 0, 1$

4. $2m = -6n - 5$; $n = 1, 2, 3$

5. $8n = -3m + 1$; $n = -2, 2, 4$

6. $4n - 6m = -2$; $n = -2, 0, 2$

7. $-5n = 13 - 3m$; $n = -3, 0, 3$

8. $10m + 6n = 12$; $n = -2, -1, 0$

Solve each equation for *x*.

9. $fx - gx = h$

10. $qx + x = r$

11. $m = \dfrac{x + n}{p}$

12. $d = f + fx$

13. $-3(x + n) = x$

14. $\dfrac{x - 4}{y + 2} = 5$

Solve each problem. Round to the nearest tenth, if necessary. Use 3.14 for pi.

15. What is the width of a rectangle with length 14 cm and area 161 cm^2?

16. What is the radius of a circle with circumference 13 ft?

17. A rectangle has perimeter 182 in. and length 52 in. What is the width?

18. A triangle has base 7 m and area 17.5 m^2. What is the height?

2-5 Practice (continued)
Form G

Literal Equations and Formulas

Solve each problem. Round to the nearest tenth, if necessary.

19. To find the average number of points per game a player scores, use the formula Points Per Game = $\frac{\text{Total Points}}{\text{Games}}$. Find the number of games a player has played if she has scored a total of 221 points and is averaging 17 points per game.

20. Joan drives 333.5 miles before she has to buy gas. Her car gets 29 miles per gallon. How many gallons of gas did the car start out with?

21. Stan is purchasing sub-flooring for a kitchen he is remodeling. The area of the floor is 180 ft^2 and the width of the kitchen is 12 ft. What is the length of the sub-floor?

Solve each equation for the given variable.

22. $4k + mn = n - 3; n$

23. $\frac{c}{d} + 2 = \frac{f}{g}; c$

24. $3ab - 2bc = 12; c$

25. $z = \left(\frac{x + y}{3}\right)w; y$

26. $-3(m - 2n) = 5m; m$

27. $A = \frac{1}{2}bcd + bc; d$

28. A room with width w, length l, and height h with four walls needs to be painted.

   a. Write a formula for the area that needs to be painted not accounting for doors or windows.

   b. Rewrite the formula to find h in terms of A, l, and w.

   c. If l is 18 ft, w is 14 ft and A is 512 ft^2, what is the height of the room?

   d. Reasoning Suppose l is equal to w. Write a formula for A in terms of w and h.

2-5 Practice   Form K

Literal Equations and Formulas

Solve each equation for y. Then find the value of y for each value of x.

1. $y + 5x = 6; x = -1, 0, 1$

2. $8x - 4y = -12; x = -3, -1, 1$

3. $-3y = 2x - 9; x = -3, 0, 3$

4. $5x = -y + 6; x = 1, 2, 3$

5. $6y = -3x + 12; x = -4, -2, 0$

6. $-5y + 10x = 5; x = -2, 0, 2$

Solve each equation for p.

7. $xp + yp = z$

8. $n = \dfrac{p - k}{j}$

9. $a = b + cp$

10. $\dfrac{p + 3}{m} = -1$

Solve each problem. Round to the nearest tenth, if necessary. Use 3.14 for π.

11. What is the width of a rectangle with length 25 in. and area 375 in.^{2}?

12. What is the radius of a circle with circumference 5 cm?

13. A triangle has base 15 ft and area 60 ft^2. What is the height?

2-5

Practice (continued)

Literal Equations and Formulas

Solve each problem. Round to the nearest tenth, if necessary.

14. In baseball, a player's batting average is calculated by using the formula
    Average $= \dfrac{\text{Hits}}{\text{At Bats}}$. Find the number of times a player has batted if he has
    24 hits and a batting average of approximately 0.320.

15. Dan drove 512 miles in 8 hours. What was his average speed for the trip?

Solve each equation for the given variable.

16. $-2z - xy = x + 7$ for x

17. $\dfrac{a}{b} - 8 = \dfrac{c}{d}$ for a

18. $6qr + 7rs - 2st = -9$ for r

19. $p = \left(\dfrac{m + n}{-5}\right)$ for n

20. A large box shaped like a rectangular prism needs to be painted.
    a. Write a formula for the area A to paint in terms of length l, width w, and height h.

    b. Rewrite the formula to find l in terms of A, h, and w.

    c. If h is 36 in., w is 28 in. and A is 6112 in.^{2}, what is the length of the prism?

Name _____ Class _____ Date _____

2-5

Standardized Test Prep

Literal Equations and Formulas

Multiple Choice

For Exercises 1–5, choose the correct letter.

1. What is the value of the expression $-2(3x - 2) + x + 9$ when $x = -3$?
   A. -16 **B.** -2 **C.** 28   **D.** 34

2. What is the value of the expression $6m + m - 4(-2m + 1 - m)$ when $m = -8$?
   F. -156 **G.** -92 **H.** -44 **I.** 36

3. What is the solution of $2d = \dfrac{a - b}{b - c}$ when you solve for a?
   A. $2d - b + c + b$
   B. $\dfrac{2d + b}{b - c}$
   C. $\dfrac{2d}{b - c} + b$
   D. $2d(b - c) + b$

4. A triangle has area 49.5 cm^2. If the base of the triangle is 9 cm, what is the height of the triangle?
   F. 5.5 cm   **G.** 11 cm   **H.** 222.75 cm   **I.** 445.5 cm

5. A circle has circumference 10.99 yd. What is the radius of the circle? Round to the nearest tenth if necessary. (Use 3.14 for π.)
   A. 1.8 yd   **B.** 3.5 yd   **C.** 7 yd   **D.** 34.5 yd

Short Response

6. The formula for the circumference of a circle is $C = 2\pi r$, where r is the radius of the circle.
   a. What is the formula when solved for r?
   b. What is the radius of a circle with a circumference of 37.7 m? Round to the nearest tenth if necessary.

2-5   Enrichment

Literal Equations and Formulas

Celsius (used in other countries) and Fahrenheit (used is the U.S.) are the two most commonly used scales for measuring temperature. Water freezes at 0°C and at 32°F. The boiling point of water is 100°C and 212°F.

To convert temperature from Celsius to Fahrenheit, you can use the formula $\frac{9}{5}C + 32 = F$, where C is degrees Celsius and F is degrees Fahrenheit.

1. Solve the above formula for C to find a formula you can use to convert degrees Fahrenheit to Celsius.

Use the formulas above for Exercises 2–6.

2. Convert 45°C to F.   3. Convert 45°F to C.

4. Convert 20°F to C.   5. Convert 110°C to F.

6. Sherry lives in Baltimore and is pen pals with Lynn who lives in England. Lynn tells Sherry that the average temperature for the past week in May was 25°C. Sherry asked Lynn if she still needed her winter coat. What was Lynn's reply? Explain.

7. The formula for the volume of a pyramid is $V = \frac{Bh}{3}$ where B is the area of the base and h is the height of the pyramid. Solve for h.

8. Use the formula you found in question 7 to determine the height of a pyramid whose volume is 5 cm^3 and the area of the base is 3 cm^2.

2-5 Reteaching

Literal Equations and Formulas

A literal equation is an equation that involves two or more variables. When you work with literal equations, you can use the methods you have learned in this chapter to isolate any particular variable. To solve for specific values of a variable, simply substitute the values into your equation and simplify.

Problem

What is the solution of $4x - 5y = 3$ for y? What is the value of y when $x = 10$?

$4x - 5y - 4x = 3 - 4x$	To get the y-term by itself on the left side, subtract $4x$ from each side.
$-5y = -4x + 3$	Simplify.
$\dfrac{-5y}{-5} = \dfrac{-4x + 3}{-5}$	Divide each side by -5 since y is being multiplied by -5 on the left side. This isolates y.
$y = \dfrac{4}{5}x - \dfrac{3}{5}$	Simplify by dividing each term by -5. Notice, this changes the sign of each term.
$y = \dfrac{4}{5}(10) - \dfrac{3}{5}$	To find the value of y when $x = 10$, substitute 10 in for x.
$y = 7\dfrac{2}{5}$	Simplify by multiplying first, then subtracting.

When you rewrite literal equations, you may have to divide by a variable or variable expression. When you do so in this lesson, assume that the variable or variable expression is not equal to zero because division by zero is not defined.

Problem

Solve the equation $ab - bc = cd$ for b.

$b(a - c) = cd$	Since b is a factor of each term on the left side, it can be factored out using the Distributive Property.
$\dfrac{b(a - c)}{a - c} = \dfrac{cd}{a - c}$	To get b by itself, divide each side by $a - c$ since b is being multiplied by $a - c$. Remember $a - c \neq 0$.
$b = \dfrac{cd}{a - c}$	Simplify.

Solve each equation for y. Then find the value of y for each value of x.

1. $y + 5x = 2; -1, 0, 1$

2. $6x = 2y - 4; 1, 2, 4$

3. $6x - 3y = -9; -2, 0, 2$

4. $4y = 5x - 8; -2, -1, 0$

5. $3y + 2x = -5; 0, 2, 3$

6. $5x = 8y - 6; -1, 0, 1$

7. $3(y - 2) + x = 1; -1, 0, 1$

8. $\dfrac{x + 2}{y - 3} = 1; -1, 0, 1$

9. $\dfrac{y + 4}{x - 5} = -3; -2, 2, 4$

2-5

Reteaching (continued)

Literal Equations and Formulas

A formula is an equation that states a relationship among quantities. Formulas are special types of literal equations. Some common formulas are shown below. Notice that some of the formulas use the same variables, but the definitions of the variables are different. For instance, r is the radius in the area and circumference of a circle and the rate in the distance formula.

Formula Name	Formula
Perimeter of a rectangle	$P = 2l + 2w$
Circumference of a circle	$C = 2\pi r$
Area of a rectangle	$A = lw$
Area of a triangle	$A = \frac{1}{2}bh$
Area of a circle	$A = \pi r^2$
Distance traveled	$d = rt$

Each of the formulas can be solved for any of the other unknowns in the equation to produce a new formula. For example, $r = \frac{C}{2\pi}$ is a formula for the radius of a circle in terms of its circumference.

Problem

What is the length of a rectangle with width 24 cm and area 624 cm^2?

$A = lw$	Formula for the area of a rectangle.
$\frac{A}{w} = \frac{lw}{w}$	Since you are trying to get l by itself, divide each side by w.
$l = \frac{A}{w}$	Simplify.
$l = \frac{624}{24}$	Substitute 624 for A and 24 for w.
$l = 26$ cm	Simplify.

Solve each problem. Round to the nearest tenth, if necessary. Use 3.14 for π.

10. A triangle has base 6 cm and area 42 cm^2. What is the height of the triangle?

11. What is the radius of a circle with circumference 56 in.?

12. A rectangle has perimeter 80 m and length 27 m. What is the width?

13. What is the length of a rectangle with area 402 ft^2 and width 12 ft?

14. What is the radius of a circle with circumference 27 in.?

2-6 ELL Support
Ratios, Rates, and Conversions

Complete the vocabulary chart by filling in the missing information.

Word or Word Phrase	Definition	Picture or Example
ratio	A *ratio* compares two numbers by division, and can be written as $\frac{a}{b}$, *a* to *b*, or *a* : *b*, where *b* does not equal zero.	4 to 6, 4 : 6 , or $\frac{4}{6}$
rate	A *rate* is a *ratio* with two quantities with different units.	**1.**
unit rate	**2.**	$\frac{7\ miles}{1\ hour}$, $\frac{\$6.50}{1\ ticket}$
conversion factor	A *conversion factor* helps you change a value in one measurement unit to a value in a different measurement unit. A *conversion factor* is a ratio of two equivalent measures in different units.	**3.**
numerator	**4.**	$\frac{24}{39}$ ←
denominator	The bottom number in a fraction is the *denominator*.	**5.**

2-6 Think About a Plan

Ratios, Rates, and Conversions

Reasoning A traveler changed $300 to euros for a trip to Germany, but the trip was canceled. Three months later, the traveler changed the euros back to dollars. Would you expect that the traveler got exactly $300 back? Explain.

Know

1. What facts do you know about the situation?

   _____

   _____

2. What circumstances would affect whether or not the traveler would receive exactly $300 back?

   _____

   _____

Need

3. What would you need to know to determine the amount of dollars the traveler would receive after three months?

   _____

   _____

4. How do you convert the amount in euros to dollars?

   _____

Plan

5. Once you have the information you need to answer the question, explain how you would determine the amount of dollars the traveler would receive in exchange for the euros.

   _____

   _____

   _____

6. Would this process change over time? Explain.

   _____

   _____

2-6 Practice   Form G
Ratios, Rates, and Conversions

Convert the given amount to the given unit.

1. 15 days; hours

2. 60 ft; yd

3. 100 meters; cm

4. 5 hr; min

5. 12 meters; ft

6. 16 in.; cm

7. 5 liters; qt

8. 2076 cm; yd

9. 15 pounds; grams

10. 25 km; cm

11. 3 mi; ft

12. 60 min; s

13. The builder measures the perimeter of the foundation to be 425 ft. He must order steel beams to install around the perimeter of the foundation. Steel must be ordered in meters. How many meters of steel should the builder order?

14. Mrs. Jacobsen purchased a 5-pound package of ground beef for $12.40. She decided to use 8 ounces each day for dinner recipes. What was the cost of ground beef per meal?

15. Car 1 drove 408 miles in 6 hours and Car 2 drove 365 miles in 5 hours during the cross-country road race. Who had the fastest average speed?

Copy and complete each statement.

16. 25 mi/hr = ___ m/min

17. 32 mi/gal = ___ km/L

18. 10 m/s = ___ ft/s

19. 14 gal/s = ___ qt/min

20. 3.5 days = ___ min

21. 100 yd = ___ m

22. 15 dollars/hr = ___ cents/min

23. 5 L/s = ___ kL/min

24. 62 in. = ___ m

25. 7 days = ___ s

2-6 Practice (continued)   *Form G*

Ratios, Rates, and Conversions

26. Which weighs more, 500 pounds or 200 kilograms?

27. Which is longer, 4000 ft or 1 kilometer?

28. Which is the better buy, 7 pounds for $8.47 or 9 pounds for $11.07? Explain.

29. A runner is running 10 miles per hour.
    a. What conversion factors should be used to convert 10 mi/hr to ft/s?

    b. How many feet per second is the runner running?

Determine if each rate is a unit rate. Explain.

30. $1.99 per pound   **31.** 100 feet per 2 seconds   **32.** 22 miles per gallon

Find each unit rate.

33. 4 pounds of green peppers cost $7.56.

34. Rahul travelled 348 miles in 6 hours.

35. Cheryl assembled 128 chairs in 16 hours.

36. Writing Suppose you want to convert feet per second to miles per hour. What conversion factors would you use? How did you determine which unit should go in the numerator and which unit should go in the denominator of the conversion factors?

37. The volume of a box is 1344 cubic inches or in^3.
    a. How many cubic inches are in one cubic foot? Justify your answer.

    b. What is the volume of the box in cubic feet? Justify your answer.

2-6

Practice

Form K

Ratios, Rates, and Conversions

Convert the given amount to the given unit.

1. 12 in.; cm   2. 528 cm; yd   3. 9 hr; min

4. 12 meters; cm   5. 8 liters; qt   6. 7 days; hours

7. 10 pounds; grams   8. 45 ft; yd   9. 10 meters; ft

10. A plumber needs to replace 20 feet of copper piping. When he gets to the supply store, the lengths are given in meters. How many meters of piping does he need to purchase?

11. An athletic director is laying out a rectangular soccer field to be 60 m wide and 95 m long. What are the dimensions of the field to the nearest whole yard?

Complete each statement.

12. 9 gal/s = _____ qt/min   13. 5.5 days = _____ min

14. 50 yd = _____ m   15. 10 mi/hr = _____ m/min

16. 25 mi/gal = _____ km/L   17. 5 m/s = _____ ft/s

2-6 **Practice** (continued)   *Form K*
_____

Ratios, Rates, and Conversions

18. Which weighs more, 5 ounces or 150 grams?

19. Which is longer, 5 miles or 10 kilometers?

20. Which is the better buy, 3 pounds for $8.31 or 5 pounds for $12.95? Explain.

21. A cyclist is riding 18 miles per hour.
   a. What conversion factors should be used to convert 18 mi/hr to ft/sec?

   b. How many feet per second is the cyclist riding?

Determine if each rate is a unit rate. Explain.

22. 3 liters per 60 seconds   **23.** 55 miles per hour   **24.** $15 per hour

Find each unit rate.

25. 5 pounds of apples cost $9.95.

26. The tub filled with 12 gallons of water in 5 minutes.

27. Rocky earned $102 in 8 hours.

28. Writing Suppose you want to convert pounds to kilograms. What conversion factors would you choose to use? How did you determine which units should go in the numerators and the denominators of the conversion factors?

2-6 Standardized Test Prep

Ratios, Rates, and Conversions

Multiple Choice

For Exercises 1–6, choose the correct letter.

1. Which of the following rates is a unit rate?

   A. $\frac{24 \text{ in.}}{1 \text{ yd}}$　　　**B.** $\frac{24 \text{ in.}}{2 \text{ ft}}$　　　**C.** $\frac{3 \text{ ft}}{1 \text{ yd}}$　　　**D.** $\frac{1 \text{ ft}}{12 \text{ in.}}$

2. How many centimeters are in 1 kilometer?

   F. 0.000001　　　**G.** 0.00001　　　**H.** 10,000　　　**I.** 100,000

3. How many inches are in 3 yd 2 ft?

   A. 60　　　**B.** 72　　　**C.** 132　　　**D.** 180

4. To convert miles per hour to feet per second, which conversion factor would not be used?

   F. $\frac{1 \text{ hr}}{60 \text{ min}}$　　　**G.** $\frac{1 \text{ min}}{60 \text{ sec}}$　　　**H.** $\frac{5280 \text{ ft}}{1 \text{ mi}}$　　　**I.** $\frac{1 \text{ mi}}{5280 \text{ ft}}$

5. A healthy, adult cheetah can run 110 feet per second. How fast can a cheetah run in miles per hour?

   A. 55　　　**B.** 75　　　**C.** 87　　　**D.** 161.3

6. Emmanuel was speaking with a friend from another country. His friend told him that the speed limit on most highways is 100 kilometers per hour in her country. This speed sounded fast to Emmanuel. Approximately what speed is this in miles per hour?

   F. 62 mph　　　**G.** 65 mph　　　**H.** 70 mph　　　**I.** 100 mph

Short Response

7. Samantha earns $22 per hour as a plumbing apprentice. How much does she earn per minute in cents?

   a. What conversion factors would she use?

   b. What amount does she earn per minute in cents?

2-6 Enrichment

Ratios, Rates, and Conversions

Nutritional information is placed on most food products. This data typically includes the number of calories, and the amount of protein, fat, or carbohydrates per serving. It may also include the amount of vitamins and minerals contained in the food.

Shown below are the nutrition information panels from a can of peanuts and a can of cashews. Both are dry roasted without salt.

Peanuts

Serving size . . . . 3 oz

Servings/container 4

Calories 510

Protein . . . . 21 g

Carbohydrates . . . . . . 18 g

Fat . . . . 42 g

Cashews

Serving Size . . . . 1.5 oz

Servings/container 8

Calories 240

Protein . . . . .6 g

Carbohydrates . . . . . . 13.5 g

Fat . . . . 19.5 g

1. Express the relationship of calories to ounces as a rate for the peanuts and cashews.

2. Express the relationship between grams of protein and ounces as a rate for the peanuts and cashews.

3. Express the relationship between grams of fat and ounces as a rate for the peanuts and cashews.

4. Based on your answer to Exercise 1, which product is lower in calories per ounce? How can you tell?

5. A friend wants to find products that are low in calories and fat and high in protein. Which would be the better choice for this friend—peanuts or cashews? Why?

6. What factors must be considered when comparing nutrition information labels on different food products?

2-6 Reteaching

Ratios, Rates, and Conversions

A unit rate is a rate with denominator 1. For example, $\frac{12 \text{ in.}}{1 \text{ ft}}$ is a unit rate. Unit rates can be used to compare quantities and convert units.

Problem

Which is greater, 74 inches or 6 feet?

It is helpful to convert to the same units. Conversion factors, a ratio of two equivalent measures in different units, are used to do conversions.

Multiply the original quantity by the conversion factor(s) so that units cancel out, leaving you with the desired units.

$$6 \cancel{\text{ft}} \times \frac{12 \text{ in}}{1 \cancel{\text{ft}}} = 72 \text{ in.}$$

Since 72 in. is less than 74 in., 74 in. is greater than 6 ft.

Rates, which involve two different units, can also be converted. Since rates involve two different units, you must multiply by two conversion factors to change both of the units.

Problem

Jared's car gets 26 mi per gal. What is his fuel efficiency in kilometers per liter? You need to convert miles to kilometers and gallons to liters. This will involve multiplying by two conversion factors.

There are 1.6 km in 1 mi. The conversion factor is either $\frac{1.6 \text{ km}}{1 \text{ mi}}$ or $\frac{1 \text{ mi}}{1.6 \text{ km}}$.

Since miles is in the numerator of the original quantity, use $\frac{1.6 \text{ km}}{1 \text{ mi}}$ as the conversion factor so that miles will cancel.

$$26 \frac{\cancel{\text{mi}}}{\text{gal}} \times \frac{1.6 \text{ km}}{1 \cancel{\text{mi}}}$$

There are 3.8 L in 1 gal. The conversion factor is either $\frac{3.8 \text{ L}}{1 \text{ gal}}$ or $\frac{1 \text{ gal}}{3.8 \text{ L}}$.

Since gallons is in the denominator of the original quantity, use $\frac{1 \text{ gal}}{3.8 \text{ L}}$ as the conversion factor so that gallons will cancel.

$$26 \frac{\cancel{\text{mi}}}{\cancel{\text{gal}}} \times \frac{1.6 \text{ km}}{1 \cancel{\text{mi}}} \times \frac{1 \cancel{\text{gal}}}{3.8 \text{ L}} \approx 10.9 \frac{\text{km}}{\text{L}}$$

Jared's vehicle gets 10.9 kilometers per liter.

2-6

Reteaching (continued)

Ratios, Rates, and Conversions

Exercises

Convert the given amount to the given unit.

1. 12 hours; minutes   2. 1000 cm; km   3. 45 ft; yd

4. 32 cups; gallons   5. 30 m; cm   6. 15 lbs; kilograms

7. 42 in.; cm   8. 10 miles; km   9. 25 ft; in.

10. Serra rode 15 mi in 1.5 hr. Phaelon rode 38 mi in 3.5 h. Justice rode 22 mi in 2.25 hr. Who had the fastest average speed?

11. Mr. Hintz purchased 12 gallons of drinking water for his family for $14.28. He knows that this should last for 2 weeks. What is the average cost per day for drinking water for the family?

12. The unit price for a particular herb is 49 cents for 6 ounces. What is the price of the herb in dollars per pound?

Copy and complete each statement.

13. $45 \text{ mi/h} = \underline{\hspace{1cm}} \text{ft/s}$ 14. $7 \text{ g/s} = \underline{\hspace{1cm}} \text{kg/min}$ 15. $50 \text{ cents/min} = \underline{\hspace{1cm}} \text{\$/h}$

16. $22 \text{ m/h} = \underline{\hspace{1cm}} \text{cm/s}$ 17. $15 \text{ km/min} = \underline{\hspace{1cm}} \text{mi/h}$ 18. $6 \text{ gal/min} = \underline{\hspace{1cm}} \text{qt/h}$

19. **Writing** Describe the conversion factor you would use to convert feet to miles. How do you determine which units to place in the numerator and the denominator?

20. **Writing** Describe a unit rate. How do you determine the unit rate if the rate is not given as a unit rate. Illustrate using an example.

2-7 ELL Support

Solving Proportions

The column on the left shows the steps used to solve a proportion. Use the column on the left to answer each question in the column on the right.

Problem **Solving With a Proportion**	**1.** Read the title of the Problem. What does the title tell you?
Twelve of the thirty-two students in the class voted to have the test on Thursday. What percent of the class voted for Thursday?	_____ _____
Write a proportion. $\frac{12}{32} = \frac{c}{100}$	**2.** What is a proportion? _____
Write the cross products. $12 \cdot 100 = 32 \cdot c$	**3.** What does writing the cross products mean? _____ _____
Simplify. $1200 = 32c$	**4.** What operation does $32c$ show? _____
Divide each side by 32. $\frac{1200}{32} = \frac{32c}{32}$	**5.** Why do you divide each side by 32? _____ _____
Simplify $1200 \div 32 = 37.5$. $37.5 = c$	**6.** Why can you write $\frac{1200}{32}$ as $1200 \div 32$? _____
Round to the nearest percent. $38 \approx c$	**7.** What does the symbol $\approx$ stand for? _____
Answer the question asked. Approximately 38% of the class voted for Thursday.	**8.** Why does the answer use the word approximately? _____ _____

Name _____ Class _____ Date _____

2-7 Think About a Plan

Solving Proportions

Video Downloads A particular computer takes 15 min to download a 45-min TV show. How long will it take the computer to download a 2-hour movie?

Understanding the Problem

1. What facts do you know about the situation?

_____

_____

_____

2. Are the units given in such a way that the numerators and the denominators of the proportion have the same units? If so, what are the units? If not, which units need to be converted?

_____

_____

_____

Planning the Solution

3. If unit conversions are necessary, use conversion factors to convert the units. Show your work.

_____

_____

4. Write a proportion that can be used to determine the length of time necessary for the computer to download the movie.

_____

Getting an Answer

5. Solve the proportion you wrote in Step 4 to find how long it will take the computer to download the movie.

Name _____ Class _____ Date _____

2-7 Practice   Form G
Solving Proportions

Solve each proportion using the Multiplication Property of Equality.

1. $\frac{3}{2} = \frac{n}{6}$

2. $\frac{1}{5} = \frac{t}{3}$

3. $\frac{g}{3} = \frac{10}{9}$

4. $\frac{m}{4} = \frac{6}{5}$

5. $\frac{7}{6} = \frac{b}{2}$

6. $\frac{2}{9} = \frac{j}{18}$

7. $\frac{z}{3} = \frac{5}{4}$

8. $\frac{11}{12} = \frac{w}{15}$

9. $\frac{19}{10} = \frac{c}{23}$

Solve each proportion using the Cross Products Property.

10. $\frac{1}{4} = \frac{x}{10}$

11. $\frac{3}{n} = \frac{2}{3}$

12. $\frac{r}{12} = \frac{3}{4}$

13. $\frac{5}{y} = \frac{-3}{5}$

14. $\frac{-3}{4} = \frac{k}{16}$

15. $\frac{22}{a} = \frac{-6}{5}$

16. $\frac{15}{9} = \frac{8}{z}$

17. $\frac{11}{5} = \frac{q}{-6}$

18. $\frac{f}{-18} = \frac{6}{-12}$

19. The windows on a building are proportional to the size of the building. The height of each window is 18 in., and the width is 11 in. If the height of the building is 108 ft, what is the width of the building?

20. Eric is planning to bake approximately 305 cookies. If 3 pounds of cookie dough make 96 cookies, how many pounds of cookie dough should he make?

21. On a map, the distance between Sheila's house and Shardae's house is 6.75 inches. According to the scale, 1.5 inches represents 5 miles. How far apart are the houses?

2-7 Practice (continued)

Form G

Solving Proportions

Solve each proportion using any method.

22. $\dfrac{n+4}{-6} = \dfrac{8}{2}$

23. $\dfrac{10}{4} = \dfrac{z-8}{16}$

24. $\dfrac{3}{t+7} = \dfrac{5}{-8}$

25. $\dfrac{x-3}{3} = \dfrac{x+4}{4}$

26. $\dfrac{3}{n+1} = \dfrac{4}{n+4}$

27. $\dfrac{4d+1}{d+9} = \dfrac{-3}{-2}$

28. Sixty-two students, out of 100 surveyed, chose pizza as their favorite lunch item. If the school has 1250 students, how many students would likely say that pizza is their favorite if the survey is a fair representation of the student body?

29. The senior class is taking a trip to an amusement park. They received a special deal where for every 3 tickets they purchased they received one free ticket. 3 tickets cost $53.25. The total purchase of tickets cost $1384.50. How many tickets did they receive?

Solve each proportion.

30. $\dfrac{x-1}{2} = \dfrac{x-2}{3}$

31. $\dfrac{2n+1}{n+2} = \dfrac{5}{4}$

32. $\dfrac{3}{2b-1} = \dfrac{2}{b+2}$

33. Open-Ended Give one example of a proportion. Describe the means and the extremes of the proportion. Explain how you know it is a proportion. Give one non-example of a proportion. Explain how you know it is not a proportion.

2-7 Practice

Form K

Solving Proportions

Solve each proportion using the Multiplication Property of Equality.

1. $\frac{3}{4} = \frac{a}{12}$

2. $\frac{1}{3} = \frac{m}{21}$

3. $\frac{x}{5} = \frac{2}{3}$

4. $\frac{f}{24} = \frac{3}{8}$

5. $\frac{9}{7} = \frac{z}{126}$

6. $\frac{3}{10} = \frac{b}{14}$

Solve each proportion using the Cross Products Property.

7. $\frac{2}{5} = \frac{k}{18}$

8. $\frac{4}{n} = \frac{6}{7}$

9. $\frac{q}{-15} = \frac{1}{3}$

10. $\frac{4}{d} = \frac{-1}{4}$

11. $\frac{-13}{15} = \frac{k}{-5}$

12. $\frac{-14}{h} = \frac{-2}{5}$

13. On a scale drawing of a park, the length of a trail is 12 cm from the playground to the pond and 15 cm from the pond to the parking lot. If the actual length of the trail from the pond to the parking lot is 60 m, what is the actual length of the trail between the playground and the pond?

14. Jennifer is ordering cake for her wedding reception. If one cake will feed 18 people, how many cakes does she need to order for 150 people?

2-7 Practice (continued) Form K
Solving Proportions

15. Julie is drawing a map of the town. She knows that City Hall is 3 miles down Main St. from the fire station. If the scale for the map is 0.25 in.: 0.5 miles, how long should Main St. be between City Hall and the fire station on the map?

Solve each proportion using any method.

16. $\frac{2}{j+3} = \frac{4}{5}$

17. $\frac{p+1}{6} = \frac{6}{11}$

18. $\frac{-4}{5} = \frac{3}{z-5}$

19. $\frac{15-b}{6} = \frac{-2}{3}$

20. A furniture factory makes 5 recliners for every 2 couches. If the factory makes a total of 154 recliners and couches in a day, how many recliners were made?

21. On the football team, two out of every seven players are seniors. If the team has 84 players, how many of the players are not seniors?

Solve each proportion.

22. $\frac{5}{n-12} = \frac{-1}{n}$

23. $\frac{4v-2}{8v} = \frac{2}{3}$

24. Writing Describe two different ways to solve $\frac{5}{6} = \frac{x}{24}$. Demonstrate both methods.

Name _____ Class _____ Date _____

2-7 Standardized Test Prep
Solving Proportions

Multiple Choice

For Exercises 1–5, choose the correct letter.

1. What is the solution to the proportion $\frac{3}{5} = \frac{x}{10}$?

   A. $\frac{10}{3}$ **B.** 6   **C.** 10   **D.** 150

2. What is the solution to the proportion $\frac{x-1}{x} = \frac{2}{3}$?

   F. -2 **G.** 0   **H.** 2   **I.** 3

3. There are 105 members of the high school marching band. For every 3 boys there are 4 girls. Which proportion represents how many boys are in the marching band?

   A. $\frac{3}{7} = \frac{b}{105}$ **B.** $\frac{3}{4} = \frac{b}{105}$ **C.** $\frac{4}{7} = \frac{b}{105}$ **D.** $\frac{7}{3} = \frac{b}{105}$

4. A baker is making bread dough. He uses 3 cups of flour for every 8 ounces of water. How many cups of flour will he use if he uses 96 ounces of water?

   F. 4   **G.** 12   **H.** 32   **I.** 36

5. Mr. Carter offered to stay after school for an extra help session, and $\frac{2}{11}$ of his students stayed for the session. If there were 24 students that stayed for the help session, how many students does Mr. Carter teach throughout the day?

   A. 100   **B.** 121   **C.** 132   **D.** 144

Extended Response

6. Elisabeth goes on a 5 mile run each Saturday. Her run typically takes her 45 minutes. She wants to increase this distance to 7 miles. Determine the proportion you use to find the time it would take her to run 7 miles. Solve the proportion. What proportion can be used to determine the time it takes for her to run a marathon, which is approximately 26 miles? What is her time?

2-7

Enrichment

Solving Proportions

When dealing with right triangles, certain ratios are formed called trigonometric ratios. They are formed by examining various sides in relation to the angles. A commonly used triangle is the 30°-60°-90° triangle shown at the right. The hypotenuse is the side opposite the 90° angle. The other two sides are called sides opposite or adjacent to respective angles in the triangle.

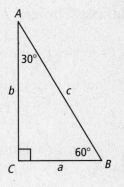

Side a is opposite to angle A and adjacent to angle B. Side b is opposite to angle b and adjacent to angle A.

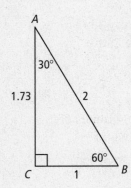

All 30°-60°-90° triangles are proportional, so the relationships shown in the triangle at the left can be used to determine missing lengths of any other 30°-60°-90° triangle provided you are given one side.

Use the relationships shown and proportions to determine the length of the other two sides.

1.

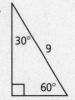

2.

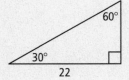

3.

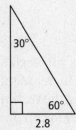

4.

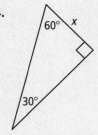

2-7

Reteaching
Solving Proportions

A proportion is an equation that states that two ratios are equal. If a quantity in a proportion is unknown, you can solve a proportion to find the unknown quantity as shown below.

Problem

What is the solution of $\frac{3}{4} = \frac{x}{14}$?

There are two methods for solving proportions—using the Multiplication Property of Equality and the Cross Products Property.

1) The multiplication Property of Equality says that you can multiply both sides of an equation by the same number without changing the value.

$$\frac{3}{4} = \frac{x}{14}$$

$14\left(\frac{3}{4}\right) = \left(\frac{x}{14}\right)14$ To isolate x, multiply each side by 14.

$\frac{42}{4} = x$ Simplify.

$10.5 = x$ Divide 42 by 4.

2) The Cross Products Property says that you can multiply diagonally across the proportion and these products are equal.

$$\frac{3}{4} = \frac{x}{14}$$

$(4)(x) = (3)(14)$ Multiply diagonally across the proportion.

$4x = 42$ Multiply.

$\frac{4x}{4} = \frac{42}{4}$ To isolate x, divide each side by 4.

$x = 10.5$ Simplify.

Real world situations can be modeled using proportions.

Problem

A bakery can make 6 dozen donuts every 21 minutes. How many donuts can the bakery make in 2 hours?

A proportion can be used to answer this question. It is key for you to set up the proportion with matching units in both numerators and both denominators.

For this problem, you know that 2 hours is 120 minutes and 6 dozen is 72 donuts.

Correct:

$$\frac{72 \text{ donuts}}{21 \text{ min}} = \frac{x \text{ donuts}}{120 \text{ min}}$$

Incorrect:

$$\frac{72 \text{ donuts}}{21 \text{ min}} = \frac{120 \text{ min}}{x \text{ donuts}}$$

2-7   **Reteaching** (continued)

Solving Proportions

This proportion can be solved using the Multiplication Property of Equality or the Cross Products Property.

Problem

Solve this proportion using the cross products.

$$\frac{72 \text{ donuts}}{21 \text{ min}} = \frac{x \text{ donuts}}{120 \text{ min}}$$

$21x = (72)(120)$ Cross Products Property

$21x = 8640$ Multiply.

$\frac{21x}{21} = \frac{8640}{21}$ Divide each side by 21.

$x = 411.43$ Simplify.

Since you cannot make 0.43 donuts, the correct answer is 411 donuts.

Exercises

Solve each proportion using the Multiplication Property of Equality.

1. $\frac{3}{4} = \frac{n}{7}$ **2.** $\frac{1}{3} = \frac{t}{10}$ **3.** $\frac{n}{5} = \frac{8}{20}$

4. $\frac{z}{6} = \frac{9}{8}$ **5.** $\frac{15}{5} = \frac{a}{11}$ **6.** $\frac{7}{2} = \frac{d}{8}$

Solve each proportion using the Cross Products Property.

7. $\frac{3}{5} = \frac{b}{8}$ **8.** $\frac{12}{m} = \frac{8}{3}$ **9.** $\frac{z}{2} = \frac{9}{6}$

10. $\frac{14}{v} = \frac{7}{3}$ **11.** $\frac{-4}{-9} = \frac{f}{-12}$ **12.** $\frac{13}{h} = \frac{2}{-6}$

13. A cookie recipe calls for a half cup of chocolate chips per 3 dozen cookies. How many cups of chocolate chips should be used for 10 dozen cookies?

Solve each proportion using any method.

14. $\frac{x-3}{-2} = \frac{4}{5}$ **15.** $\frac{12}{10} = \frac{y+6}{13}$ **16.** $\frac{5}{x-3} = \frac{2}{-6}$

2-8

ELL Support

Proportions and Similar Figures

Concept List

Cross Products Property	is congruent to	is similar to
length	proportion	ratio
scale	scale model	similar figures

Choose the concept from the list above that best represents the item in each box.

1. $24x = 10(18)$	**2.** ~	**3.** $\dfrac{AB}{FG} = \dfrac{BC}{GH}$
4. $1\,\text{cm} : 12\,\text{m}$	**5.** 	**6.** $\overline{RT}$
7. $\cong$	**8.** $\dfrac{16}{13}$	**9.**

2-8

Think About a Plan

Proportions and Similar Figures

Trucks A model of a trailer is shaped like a rectangular prism and has a width of 2 in., a length of 9 in., and a height of 4 in. The scale of the model is 1 : 34. How many times the volume of the model of the trailer is the volume of the actual trailer?

Understanding the Problem

1. What is the formula you use to find the volume of a rectangular prism?

   _____

2. Using the scale, how can we find the dimensions of the actual trailer?

   _____

   _____

Planning the Solution

3. What is the volume of the model?

   _____

   _____

4. Write three proportions that can be used to determine the actual length, height, and width of the trailer. Solve the proportions.

   _____

   _____

   _____

   _____

5. What is the volume of the actual trailer?

   _____

   _____

Getting an Answer

6. How many times the volume of the model of the trailer is the volume of the actual trailer? Justify your answer.

   _____

   _____

2-8 Practice

Form G

Proportions and Similar Figures

The figures in each pair are similar. Identify the corresponding sides and angles.

1. $\triangle ABC \sim \triangle DEF$

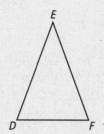

2. $QRST \sim UVWX$

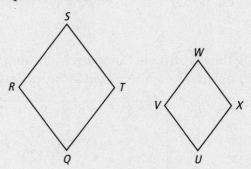

The figures in each pair are similar. Find the missing length.

3.

4.

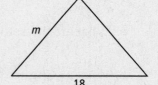

5.

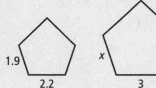

6.

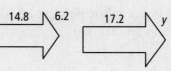

The scale of a map is 0.5 in. : 20 mi. Find the actual distance corresponding to each map distance.

7. 2 in.

8. 3.5 in.

9. 4.75 in.

10. A museum has a wax sculpture of a historical village. The scale is 1.5 : 8. If the height of a hut in the sculpture is 5 feet, how tall was the original hut to the nearest whole foot?

11. On a map, the length of a river is 4.75 in. The actual length of the river is 247 miles. What is the scale of the map?

2-8 **Practice** (continued) Form G

Proportions and Similar Figures

12. Sammy is constructing a model bridge out of sticks. The actual bridge is 1320 ft long. He wants the scale of his bridge to be 1 : 400. How long should the model be?

13. The Finish-Line Company is drawing up plans for a room addition shown below. The addition will include a large bedroom with a bathroom as shown.

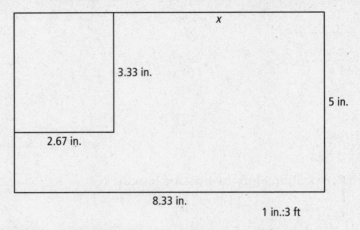

a. What are the actual dimensions of the room addition?

b. What are the actual dimensions of the bathroom?

c. What is the actual length of the exterior wall between the end of the room addition and the bathroom wall? This length is represented by x.

14. **Writing** Are all right triangles similar? Explain your answer.

15. **Writing** A pizza shop sells small 6 in. pizzas and medium 12 in. pizzas. Should the medium pizzas cost twice as much as the small pizzas because they are twice the size? Explain.

2-8

Practice

Form K

Proportions and Similar Figures

The figures in each pair are similar. Identify the corresponding sides and angles.

1. $ABCD \sim EFGH$

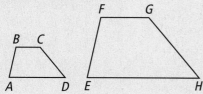

2. $\triangle MNO \sim \triangle PQR$

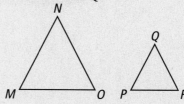

The figures in each pair are similar. Find the missing length.

3.

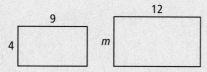

4.

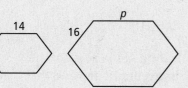

5.

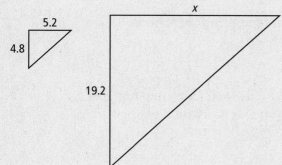

2-8

Practice (continued)

Proportions and Similar Figures

The scale of a map is 0.25 cm : 15 km. Find the actual distance corresponding to each map distance.

6. 0.75 cm

7. 2 cm

8. 3.5 cm

9. 5.25 cm

10. For a celebration a town is going to pass out miniature replicas of the town's bell. The replicas are 9 in. tall. If the scale of the replica is 1 in. : 0.5 ft, how tall is the actual bell?

11. An architect created a scale model of what a college campus will look like once construction is finished. The scale for the model is 2 in. : 25 ft. The tallest building in the model is 10 in. tall. How tall is the actual building?

12. A model of a golf course says that hole #9 is 175 yards long. If the scale of the model is 2 in. : 20 yards, how many inches are there between the tee and the hole on the model?

13. Open-Ended Give an example of similar figures in your school.

14. Reasoning You are given two similar triangles. You know that one pair of corresponding sides is equal. What do you know about the other sides? Explain.

2-8

Standardized Test Prep
Proportions and Similar Figures

Multiple Choice

For Exercises 1–4, choose the correct letter.

1. The distance between Capeton and Jonesville is 80 miles. The scale on the map is 0.75 in. : 10 miles. How far apart are the cities on the map?
   A. 6 in.   **B.** 60 in.   **C.** 600 in.   **D.** 1067 in.

2. The floor plan of a room has a scale of 2.5 in.: 35 ft. In the drawing, the length of the room is 8 in. and the width of the room is 6 in. What is the perimeter of the actual room?
   F. 84 ft   **G.** 112 ft   **H.** 196 ft   **I.** 392 ft

3. The figures are similar. What is the missing length?

   A. 9.33 cm
   B. 5.4 cm
   C. 6 cm
   D. 21 cm

   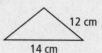 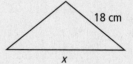

4. A model car is constructed with a scale of 1 : 15. If the actual car is 12 feet long, which proportion represents the length x of the model car?
   F. $\frac{1}{15} = \frac{x}{12}$ **G.** $\frac{1}{15} = \frac{12}{x}$ **H.** $\frac{12}{15} = \frac{1}{x}$ **I.** $\frac{1}{12} = \frac{15}{x}$

Short Response

5. The scale of a map is 0.5 in. : 25 mi. The actual distance between two cities is 725 mi. Write a proportion that represents the relationship. How far apart will the cities be on the map?

2-8   Enrichment

Proportions and Similar Figures

You are an executive who has been given the privilege of designing your floor of the office building. Below is the outline of the floor plan for your floor. There are a few things shown that cannot be moved because they affect the other floors of the building.

The plan is drawn to a scale 1 in. : 18 ft and each unit on the grid represents 0.3 in.

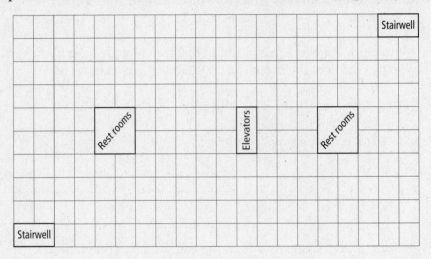

1. What are the actual dimensions of the entire office building?

2. What is the actual size of the restrooms? elevators? stairwells?

3. You design the following on your floor: 2 break rooms, 2 copier rooms, 10 executive offices that are at least 18 ft by 12 ft, and enough cubicles (minimum size of 6 ft by 6 ft) for 50 employees. Draw each of the rooms to scale on the grid shown above. Label your drawings.

4. What are the actual dimensions of each of the rooms you designed?

5. The break room has ceramic tile covering the floor. How many square yards of tile is there in the break room?

6. Describe two ways to compute the actual area of any room on the floor plan.

2-8 Reteaching

Proportions and Similar Figures

In similar figures, the measures of corresponding angles are equal, and the ratios of corresponding side lengths are equal. It is important to be able to identify the corresponding parts in similar figures.

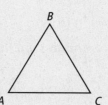 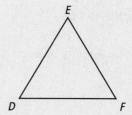

Since $\angle A \cong \angle D$, $\angle B \cong \angle E$, and $\angle C \cong \angle F$, $\frac{AB}{DE} = \frac{BC}{EF}$, $\frac{AB}{DE} = \frac{AC}{DF}$. This fact can help you to find missing lengths.

Problem

What is the missing length in the similar figures?

First, determine which sides correspond. The side with length 14 corresponds to the side with length 16. The side with length x corresponds to the side with length 12. These can be set into a proportion.

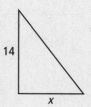 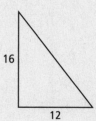

$\frac{14}{16} = \frac{x}{12}$	Write a proportion using corresponding lengths.
$(16)(x) = (14)(12)$	Cross Products Property
$16x = 168$	Multiply.
$x = 10.5$	Divide each side by 16 and simplify.

Exercises

The figures in each pair are similar. Identify the corresponding sides and angles.

1.

2.

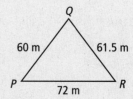

2-8 **Reteaching** (continued)

Proportions and Similar Figures

Exercises

The figures in each pair are similar. Find the missing length.

3.

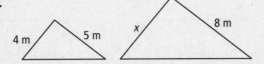

4.

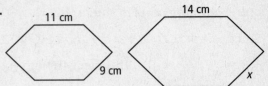

5.

6.

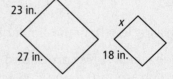

Problem

A map shows the distance between two towns is 3.5 inches where the scale on the map is 0.25 in. : 5 mi. What is the actual distance between the towns?

Map scale: $\dfrac{\text{map distance}}{\text{actual distance}}$

If you let x be the actual distance between the towns, you can set up and solve a the proportion to answer the question.

$$\frac{0.25 \text{ in.}}{5 \text{ mi}} = \frac{3.5 \text{ in.}}{x \text{ mi}}$$

$$0.25x = 17.5$$

$$x = 70$$

The towns are 70 miles apart.

Exercises

The scale of a map is 1.5 in. : 50 mi. Find the actual distance corresponding to each map distance.

7. 10 in.   8. 4.25 in.   9. 6.75 in.

10. The blueprints of an octagonal shaped hot tub are drawn with a 1 in. : 5 ft scale. In the drawing the sides are 3.5 inches long. What is the perimeter of the hot tub?

2-9

ELL Support

Percents

Use the list below to complete the diagram.

$12 = p\% \cdot 36$	$\dfrac{a}{b} = \dfrac{p}{100}$	$l = 45(0.04)6$
$\dfrac{3}{4} = \dfrac{p}{100}$	$l = prt$	$a = p\% \cdot b$

The Percent Proportion	The Percent Equation	Simple Interest Formula
_____	_____	_____
_____	_____	_____

2-9

Think About a Plan

Percents

Finance A savings account earns simple interest at a rate of 6% per year. Last year the account earned $10.86 in interest. What was the balance in the account at the beginning of last year?

Understanding the Problem

1. What is the formula for finding simple interest?

_____

2. What values are given in terms of the formula you wrote in Step 1?

_____

_____

Planning the Solution

3. Substitute the given values into the formula for simple interest.

_____

Getting an Answer

4. Solve for the unknown value.

_____

_____

5. Is your answer reasonable? Explain.

_____

_____

6. What does your solution mean?

_____

_____

2-9

Practice

Form G

Percents

Find each percent.

1. What percent of 42 is 28?

2. What percent of 48 is 18?

3. What percent of 150 is 350?

4. What percent of 99 is 72?

5. What percent of 15 is 12?

6. What percent of 120 is 200?

Find each part.

7. What is 75% of 180?

8. What is 40% of 720?

9. What is 125% of 62?

10. What is 50% of 821?

11. What is 2.75% of 20?

12. What is 16.5% of 33?

13. A set of golf clubs that costs $600 are on sale for 40% off the regular price. What is the sale price of the clubs?

14. A discount store marks up the merchandise it sells by 55%. If the wholesale price of a particular item is $25, what should the retail price be set at?

15. A used car lot runs sales at the end of the year to reduce inventory. This year the sale price is 15% less than the regular price. If the regular price of a car is $12,000, what is the sale price of the car?

2-9   **Practice** (continued)   Form G
Percents

Find each base.

16. 60% of what number is 75?

17. 115% of what number is 120?

18. 15% of what number is 6.75?

19. 5% of what number is 4.1?

20. 68% of what number is 64.6?

21. 65% of what number is 577.2?

22. If you deposit $800 in a savings account that earns simple interest at a rate of 1.5% per year, how much interest will you have earned after 5 years?

23. When Marty was born, his parents deposited $5000 in a college savings account that earns simple interest at a rate of 7.25% per year. How much interest will the money have earned after 18 years?

24. You have $10,000 to deposit in a savings account that earns simple interest at a rate of 4.5% per year. How much interest will be in the account after 2 years?

Tell whether you are finding a *percent*, a *part*, or a *base*. Then solve.

25. What is 25% of 50?

26. What percent of 18 is 63?

27. What is 133% of 90?

28. What is 44% of 88?

29. What percent of 67 is 26.8?

30. 42 is 14% of what number?

2-9

Practice

Percents

Find each percent.

1. What percent of 58 is 18?

2. What percent of 36 is 27?

3. What percent of 65 is 115?

4. What percent of 45 is 42?

Find each part.

5. What is 40% of 120?

6. What is 62% of 500?

7. What is 150% of 84?

8. What is 33% of 171?

9. A pair of pants that regularly costs $55 are on sale for 35% off the regular price. What is the sale price of the pants?

10. A friend purchases items from a wholesale website and resells them on her own website. She typically marks up her merchandise 40%. If she purchased an item for $15, what price should she set for the item?

Find each base.

11. 70% of what number is 63?

12. 55% of what number is 231?

13. 165% of what number is 132?

14. 8% of what number is 1.2?

2-9

Practice (continued)

Percents

15. $13,000 is deposited into a savings account that earns simple interest at a rate of 6.5% per year. How much interest will the money have earned after 3 years?

16. Erma has $175,000 in a retirement account that earns simple interest at a rate of 9% per year. How much interest will the money have earned after 25 years?

17. A family deposited $8000 into an account six years ago. The account earned simple interest at a yearly rate. So far the total interest earned is $1200. What is the rate for the account?

Tell whether you are finding a *percent*, a *part*, or a *base*. Then solve.

18. 112 is 20% of what number?

19. What is 126% of 50?

20. What percent of 88 is 36.96?

21. What percent of 22 is 33?

22. What is 268% of 150?

23. What is 50% of 1175?

2-9

Standardized Test Prep

Percents

Multiple Choice

For Exercises 1–5, choose the correct letter.

1. What percent of 92 is 23?
   A. 0.25%   B. 4%   C. 25%   D. 400%

2. 60% of a number is 66. Which proportion best represents this relationship?
   F. $\frac{66}{b} = \frac{60}{100}$ G. $\frac{a}{66} = \frac{60}{100}$ H. $\frac{60}{b} = \frac{66}{100}$ I. $\frac{60}{66} = \frac{b}{100}$

3. A store is having a clearance sale where merchandise on the sales racks is reduced by 80% from the original price. If a jacket was originally priced at $76, what is the sale price?
   A. $15.20   B. $24.20   C. $60.80   D. $72.40

4. If you deposit $3000 in a savings account that earns simple interest at a rate of 2.5% per year, how much interest will you have earned after 4 years?
   F. $30   G. $300   H. $3000   I. $30,000

5. Five years ago you deposited a sum of money into a savings account which has earned $150 in interest. The interest rate for the account is 3% simple interest per year. How much money was originally deposited in the account?
   A. $22.50   B. $100   C. $1000   D. $10,000

Short Response

6. There are 3200 students at Martinsville High School. There are 575 students involved in athletics during the spring athletic seasons. What proportion represents the percent of students not involved in athletics during the spring season? What percent of students is not involved in athletics?

2-9 Enrichment

Percents

Compound Interest and Annual Percentage Yield

When money is invested in some types of accounts, such as savings accounts or certificates of deposit, the interest is compounded. This means that interest is paid at intervals, such as monthly, quarterly, or yearly. The interest is added to the account, and interest is then earned on the interest that has already been paid. For every $100 invested in an account paying 6% interest, compounded twice per year, the interest earned is $6.09. This represents a rate of 6.09%, because of the compounding.

The name for the effective percent earned on an account where the interest is compounded is annual percentage yield (APY). It tells what percent of an original investment you will earn in a year.

The equation that expresses this percent is APY $= \left(1 + \frac{i}{n}\right)^n - 1$, where i is the advertised interest rate (written as a decimal) and n is the number of compounding periods per year. The result is the percent, written as a decimal. Using the example above, with $i = 0.06$ and $n = 2$:

$$\text{APY} = \left(1 + \frac{0.06}{2}\right)^2 - 1$$
$$= 1.0609 - 1$$
$$= 0.0609$$
$$= 6.09\%$$

For Exercises 1–4, determine the annual percentage yield (APY).

1. 8% interest rate, 2 compounding periods per year

2. 8% interest rate, 4 compounding periods per year

3. 8% interest rate, 6 compounding periods per year

4. 8% interest rate, 12 compounding periods per year

5. What do you notice about the APY as the number of compounding periods increases?

6. What is the relationship between the interest rate and the APY when the number of compounding periods per year is 1? What does this mean?

2-9 Reteaching

Percents

Percents compare whole quantities, represented by 100%, and parts of the whole.

Problem

What percent of 90 is 27?

There are two ways presented for finding percents.

1) You can use the percent proportion $\frac{a}{b} = \frac{p}{100}$. The percent is represented by $\frac{p}{100}$. The base, b, is the whole quantity and must be the denominator of the other fraction in the proportion. The part of the quantity is represented by a.

$\frac{27}{90} = \frac{p}{100}$	Substitute given values into the percent proportion. Since you are looking for percent, p is the unknown.
$27(100) = (90)(p)$	Cross Products Property
$2700 = 90p$	Multiply.
$30 = p$	Divide each side by 90 and simplify.

27 is 30% of 90.

2) The other way to find percents is to use the percent equation. The percent equation is $a = p\% \times b$, where p is the percent, a is the part, and b is the base.

$27 = p\% \times 90$	Substitute 27 for a and 90 for b.
$0.3 = p\%$	Divide each side by 90.
$30\% = p\%$	Write the decimal as a percent.

27 is 30% of 90.

Exercises

Find each percent.

1. What percent of 125 is 50?

2. What percent of 14 is 35?

3. What percent of 24 is 18?

4. What percent of 50 is 75?

Problem

75% of 96 is what number?

In this problem you are given the percent p and the whole quantity (base) b.

$a = p\% \times b$	Write the percent equation.
$a = 75\% \times 96 = 72$	Substitute 75 for p and 96 for b. Multiply.

2-9 Reteaching (continued)

Percents

Problem

28% of what number is 42?

You are given the percent p and the partial quantity a. You are looking for the base b.

$a = p\% \times b$	Write the percent equation.
$42 = 28\% \times b$	Substitute 28 for p and 42 for a.
$42 = 0.28 \times b$	Write 28% as a decimal, 0.28.
$150 = b$	Divide each side by 0.28.

Exercises

Find each part.

5. What is 32% of 250?   **6.** What is 78% of 130?

Find each base.

7. 45% of what number is 90?   **8.** 70% of what number is 35?

Problems involving simple interest can be solved using the formula $I = Prt$, where I is the interest, P is the principal, r is the annual interest rate written as a decimal, and t is the time in years.

Problem

You deposited $2200 in a savings account that earns a simple interest rate of 2.8% per year. You want to keep the money in the account for 3 years. How much interest will you earn?

$I = Prt$	Simple Interest Formula
$I = (2200)(2.8\%)(3)$	Substitute 2200 for P, 2.8% for r, and 3 for t.
$I = 184.8$	Multiply.

You will earn $184.80 in interest.

Exercises

9. If you deposit $11,000 in a savings account that earns simple interest at a rate of 3.5% per year, how much interest will you have earned after 5 years?

10. If you deposit $500 in a savings account that earns simple interest at a rate of 4.25% per year, how much interest will you have earned after 10 years?

2-10

ELL Support

Change Expressed as a Percent

For Exercises 1–4, draw a line from each word in Column A to its definition in
Column B. The first one is done for you.

Column A

percent

1. estimate

2. markup

3. ratio

4. percent change

Column B

expresses an amount of change as a percent of an
original amount

a ratio comparing a number to 100

an approximate answer that is relatively close to an
exact amount

a comparison of two numbers by division

the difference between the selling price and the
original cost of an item: $ 50 − $ 42

For Exercises 5–7, draw a line from each word in Column A to its definition in
Column B.

A store's cost for a sweater is $32. The store sells the sweater for $40. Then the store
puts the sweater on sale for $36.

Column A

5. discount

6. amount of increase

7. percent decrease

Column B

The new amount minus the original cost.
$40 − $32 = $8

The percent a quantity decreases from its original
amount. $\frac{(\$40 - \$36)}{40} \times 100$

The difference between the original price and the
sale price. $40 − $36 = $4

2-10

Think About a Plan

Change Expressed as a Percent

Student Discounts You show your student identification at a local restaurant in order to receive a 5% discount. You spend $12 for your meal at the restaurant. How much would your meal cost without the discount?

Understanding the Problem

1. What information are you given in the problem? What are you looking to find?

   _____

   _____

2. Does this question represent an amount of increase or an amount of decrease? In general, how is the amount of increase or decrease determined?

   _____

   _____

Planning the Solution

3. What formula can you use to determine the solution?

   _____

4. Substitute values from the problem into your formula using x for the unknown value.

   _____

Getting an Answer

5. Solve for the unknown value.

   _____

   _____

6. Check your answer.

   _____

   _____

7. Is your answer reasonable? Explain.

   _____

   _____

2-10 Practice   Form G

Change Expressed as a Percent

Tell whether each percent change is an increase or decrease. Then find the percent change. Round to the nearest percent.

1. Original amount: 10
New amount: 12

2. Original amount: 72
New amount: 67

3. Original amount: 36
New amount: 68

4. Original amount: 23
New amount: 25

5. Original amount: 83
New amount: 41

6. Original amount: 19
New amount: 30

7. Original amount: 38
New amount: 45

8. Original amount: 16
New amount: 11

9. Original amount: 177
New amount: 151

10. The price of the truck was advertised as $19,900. After talking with the salesperson, Jack agreed to pay $18,200 for the truck. What is the percent decrease to the nearest percent?

11. The Ragnier's purchased a house for $357,000. They sold their home for $475,000. What was the percent increase to the nearest percent?

12. The original price for a gallon of milk is $4.19. The sale price this week for a gallon of milk is $2.99. What is the percent decrease to the nearest percent?

Find the percent error in each estimation. Round to the nearest percent.

13. You estimate that a building is 20 m tall. It is actually 23 m tall.

14. You estimate the salesman is 45 years old. He is actually 38 years old.

15. You estimate the volume of the storage room is 800 ft^3. The room's volume is actually 810 ft^3.

2-10

Practice (continued)

Change Expressed as a Percent

A measurement is given. Find the minimum and maximum possible measurements.

16. A nurse measures a newborn baby to be 22 in. long to the nearest in.

17. A bag of apples weighs 4 lbs to the nearest lb.

18. Fencing sections come in lengths of 8 ft to the nearest foot.

Find the percent change. Round to the nearest percent.

19. 16 m to $11\frac{1}{4}$ m

20. 76 ft to $58\frac{1}{2}$ ft

21. $215\frac{1}{2}$ lb to $133\frac{1}{4}$ lb

22. $42.75 to $39.99

23. $315.99 to $499.89

24. $5762.76 to $4999.99

The measured dimensions of a rectangle are given to the nearest whole unit. Find the minimum and maximum possible areas of each rectangle.

25. 4 cm by 7 cm

26. 16 ft by 15 ft

27. 5 m by 12 m

The measured dimensions of a shape or a solid are given to the nearest whole unit. Find the greatest percent error of each shape or solid.

28. The perimeter of a rectangle with length 127 ft and width 211 ft.

29. The area of a rectangle with length 14 in. and width 11 in.

30. The volume of a rectangular prism with length 22 cm, width 36 cm, and height 19 cm.

2-10 Practice

Change Expressed as a Percent

Form K

Tell whether each percent change is an increase or decrease. Then find the percent change. Round to the nearest percent.

1. Original amount: 25
New amount: 18

2. Original amount: 48
New amount: 72

3. Original amount: 178
New amount: 136

4. Original amount: 17
New amount: 15

5. Original amount: 45
New amount: 60

6. Original amount: 95
New amount: 90

7. A store sells a running suit for $35. Joey found the same suit online for $29. What is the percent decrease to the nearest percent?

8. An online auction store started the bid on an item at $19. The item sold for $49. What was the percent increase to the nearest percent?

9. The original price for a motorcycle was $11,000. The sale price this week is $9799. What is the percent decrease to the nearest percent?

Find the percent error in each estimation. Round to the nearest percent.

10. You estimate that a tree is 45 ft tall. It is actually 58 ft tall.

11. A carpenter estimates the wall is 20 ft tall. The wall is actually 18 ft tall.

2-10

Practice (continued)

Change Expressed as a Percent

Form K

A measurement is given. Find the minimum and maximum possible measurements.

12. A patient weighs 178 lb to the nearest quarter pound.

13. A board is cut to 28 in. to the nearest half in.

Find the percent change. Round to the nearest percent.

14. $158.49 to $149.99

15. $29\frac{1}{2}$ oz to $23\frac{1}{4}$ oz

16. $12\frac{1}{4}$ hr to $13\frac{1}{2}$ hr

17. 7 in. to $12\frac{1}{2}$ in.

The measured dimensions of a rectangle are given to the nearest whole unit. Find the minimum and maximum possible areas of each rectangle.

18. 25 in. by 22 in.

19. 5 m by 7 m

The measured dimensions of a shape are given to the nearest whole unit. Find the greatest percent error of each shape.

20. The perimeter of a rectangle with length 15 cm and width 21 cm.

21. The area of a triangle with base length 32 in. and height 25 in.

2-10 Standardized Test Prep
Change Expressed as a Percent

Multiple Choice

For Exercises 1–5, choose the correct letter.

1. Sam ran 3.5 miles on Saturday. On Wednesday, he ran 5.2 miles. What was his percent increase to the nearest percent?
   A. 33%   **B.** 42%   **C.** 49%   **D.** 67%

2. A department store purchases sweaters wholesale for $16. The sweaters sell retail for $35. What is the percent increase to the nearest percent?
   F. 19%   **G.** 46%   **H.** 54%   **I.** 119%

3. Josephine measured the room to be 125 ft wide and 225 ft long. What is the maximum possible area of the room?
   A. 700 ft^2 **B.** 27,950.25 ft^2 **C.** 28,125 ft^2 **D.** 28,300.25 ft^2

4. You estimate the height of the flagpole to be 16 ft tall. The actual height of the flagpole is 18 ft. Which equation can be used to determine your percent error in the estimated height?
   F. $\dfrac{16-18}{18}$ **G.** $\dfrac{|16-18|}{18}$ **H.** $\dfrac{|16-18|}{16}$ **I.** $\dfrac{16-18}{16}$

5. You estimate that a box can hold 1152 in^3. The box is actually 10.5 in. long, 10.5 in. wide, and 8 in. tall. What is the percent error in your estimation? Round to the nearest percent.
   A. 23%   **B.** 31%   **C.** 42%   **D.** 77%

Short Response

6. You measure a tub shaped as a rectangular prism to be 3 ft wide, 4 ft long, and 2.5 feet tall to the nearest half foot. What are the minimum and maximum volumes of the tub? What is the greatest possible percent error in calculating the volume of the tub?

2-10 Enrichment

Change Expressed as a Percent

A newspaper advertisement describes an end of the season sale at a store. The ad says you can take an additional 40% off coats that are already marked down 60%.

1. Marco concluded that the ad was presenting a percent change of 100%. What is wrong with Marco's conclusion?

2. Demonstrate how you determine the percent change from the original cost to the final advertised sale price of a coat costing $100. What is the percent change?

3. A bookstore is having a storewide sale where all books are 30% off the list price. There is a clearance shelf where the price is discounted an additional 50% off. What is the percent change of the final discount for books on the clearance shelf?

4. A discount warehouse buys the products it sells and marks up the price by 75%. This weekend the product is being sold for 25% off the regular price. What is the percent change from the wholesale price for this product during the sale?

5. This year there was a 35% increase in attendance for the holiday pageant over last year's attendance. Next year, the committee is planning for a 40% increase in attendance over this year's attendance. What is the percent change from last year's attendance to next year's attendance?

6. The original price of a product is $70. The original price is discounted a certain percentage, but the discount sticker has fallen off. There is a storewide additional 30% off for all merchandise. The price rings up as $36.75 at the register. Write an equation that will determine the percent of the original discount. What is the original discount?

2-10 Reteaching

Change Expressed as a Percent

A percent change occurs when the original amount changes and the change is expressed as a percent of the original amount. There are two possibilities for percent change: percent increase or perent decrease. The following formula can be used to find percents of increase/decrease.

$$\text{percent change} = \frac{\text{amount of increase or decrease}}{\text{original amount}}$$

Problem

In its first year, membership of the community involvement club was 32 members. The second and third years there were 28 members and 35 members respectively. Determine the percent change in membership each year.

From the first to the second year, the membership went down from 32 to 28 members, representing a percent decrease. The amount of decrease can be found by subtracting the new amount from the original amount.

$$\text{percent change} = \frac{\text{original amount} - \text{new amount}}{\text{original amount}}$$ Percent Change Formula for percent decrease.

$$= \frac{32 - 28}{32}$$ Substitute 32 for the original number and 28 for the new number.

$$= \frac{4}{32} = 0.125$$ Subtract. Then divide.

Membership decreased by 12.5% from the first year to the second year.

From the second to the third year, the membership increased from 28 to 35 members, representing a percent increase. The amount of increase can be found by subtracting the original amount from the new amount.

$$\text{percent change} = \frac{\text{original amount} - \text{new amount}}{\text{original amount}}$$ Percent Change Formula for percent increase.

$$= \frac{35 - 28}{28}$$ Substitute 28 for the original number and 35 for the new number.

$$= \frac{7}{32} \approx 0.22$$ Subtract. Then divide.

Membership increased by about 22% from the second year to the third year.

Exercises

Tell whether each percent change is an increase or decrease. Then find the percent change. Round to the nearest percent.

1. Original amount: 25
   New amount: 45

2. Original amount: 17
   New amount: 10

3. Original amount: 22
   New amount: 21

2-10 Reteaching (continued)

Change Expressed as a Percent

Errors can occur when making measurements or estimations. Percents can be used to compare estimated or measured values to exact values. This is called relative error. Relative error can be determined with the following formula comparing the estimated value and the actual value.

$$\text{Percent error} = \frac{|\text{measured or estimated value} - \text{actual value}|}{\text{actual value}}$$

Problem

Mrs. Desoto estimated that her class would earn an average of $126 per person for the fundraiser. When the money was counted after the fundraiser ended, each student had raised an average of $138 per person. What is the percent error?

There are two values given in this situation. The estimated value is $126 per person. The actual value that each person raised was $138.

$$\text{Percent error} = \frac{|\text{measured or estimated value} - \text{actual value}|}{\text{actual value}}$$ Percent Error Formula

$$= \frac{|126 - 138|}{138}$$ Substitute 126 for the estimated value and 138 for the actual value.

$$= \frac{|-12|}{138}$$ Subtract.

$$= \frac{12}{138}$$ $|-12| = 12$

$$\approx 0.09$$ Divide.

There was a 9% error in her estimation.

Exercises

Find the percent error in each estimation. Round to the nearest percent.

4. You estimate that your baby sister weighs 22 lbs. She is actually 26 lbs.

5. You estimate that the bridge is 60 ft long. The bridge is actually 53 ft long.

6. You estimate the rope length to be 80 ft. The rope measures 72 ft long.

7. A carpenter estimates the roof to be 375 ft^2. The rectangular roof measures 18 feet wide by 22 feet long. What is the percent error?

Chapter 2 Quiz 1

Form G

Lessons 2-1 through 2-5

Do You Know HOW?

Solve each equation. Check your answer.

1. $45 = 3b + 69$

2. $\frac{1}{3}(c - 2) = \frac{7}{3}$

Solve each equation. Justify your steps.

3. $7 - 5t = 17$

4. $5 = \frac{1}{2}v - 3$

Solve each equation. If the equation is an identity, write *identity*. If it has no solution, write *no solution*.

5. $10\left(x + \frac{1}{2}\right) = 3x + 5 + 7x$

6. $\frac{n - 1}{2} = 17$

7. $2.8p = 11.2$

Define a variable and write an equation to model each situation. Then solve.

8. The total cost for 8 bracelets, including shipping was $54. The shipping charge was $6. What was the cost of each bracelet?

9. One music download store charges a monthly fee of $10 plus $1 per song downloaded. Another music download store charges a monthly fee of $30 for all the songs you want to download.

  a. How many songs would you have to download from the first store for the cost to be the same as the second store?

  b. If you only download 15 songs per month, from which download store would you buy your music?

Do You UNDERSTAND?

10. Reasoning When solving a multi-step equation, does it matter in which order the operations are performed? Explain.

Chapter 2 Quiz 2

Form G

Lessons 2-6 through 2-10

Do You Know HOW?

Convert the given amount to the given unit.

1. 6 min; seconds

2. 112 dollars; cents

3. 3.5 lb ; ounces

Solve each proportion. Explain your reasoning.

4. $\dfrac{x + 10}{4} = \dfrac{3}{2}$

5. $\dfrac{5}{a} = \dfrac{10}{a + 1}$

In the diagram, $\triangle ABC \sim \triangle PQR$. Find each side length.

6. *BC*

7. *CA*

8. What percent of 60 is 12?

9. What is 30% of 70?

10. Your car gets 30 mpg on the highway. If gas costs $4.20 per gallon, how much does it cost to drive your car per mile?

11. A gardener has a 15 ft² garden. If she increases to a 24 ft² garden, by what percentage does she increase the area of the garden?

Do You UNDERSTAND?

12. How are ratios and proportions the same? How are they different?

13. Error Analysis The length of an object is exactly 20 cm. A student says that a measurement of 19 cm represents a percent error of 95%, while a measurement of 21 cm represents a percent error of 105%. Explain what the student did wrong. What are the correct percent errors?

Chapter 2 Chapter Test

Form G

Do You Know HOW?

Solve each proportion.

1. $\frac{2}{1.2} = \frac{5}{k}$

2. $\frac{12}{48} = \frac{g}{20}$

3. $\frac{m}{20} = \frac{5}{4}$

Solve each equation. Check your answer.

4. $7y + 5 = 3y - 31$

5. $\frac{1}{2}(t + 7) = 32$

6. $\frac{2h - 6}{6} = \frac{2}{3}$

7. A cheetah ran 300 feet in 2.92 seconds. What was the cheetah's average speed in miles per hour?

The figures are similar. Find the missing length.

8.

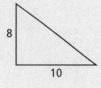
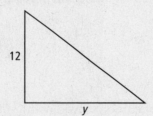

9. A tree casts a 26-ft shadow. A boy standing nearby casts a 12-ft shadow, forming similar triangles. His height is 4.5 ft. How tall is the tree?

Tell whether each percent of change is an increase or decrease. Then find the percent of change.

10. Original amount: $90

New amount: $84.50

11. Original amount: $100

New amount: $140

12. Original amount: $15

New amount: $5.50

13. Original amount: $8.50

New amount: $12.75

Chapter 2 Chapter Test (continued) Form G

Define a variable and write an equation to model each situation. Then solve.

14. An online music club sells compact discs for $13.95 each plus $1.95 shipping and handling per order. If Maria's total bill was $85.65, how many compact discs did Maria purchase?

15. Tickets to the county fair for four adults and five children cost $33.00. An adult's ticket costs $1.50 more than a child's ticket. Find the cost of an adult's ticket.

16. The scale of a map is 1 cm : 50 mi. Determine the distance between two cities that are 4.2 cm apart on the map.

17. In 1995, the price of a laser printer was $1,299. In 2002, the price of the same type of printer had dropped to $499. Find the percent of decrease.

Do You UNDERSTAND?

18. **Writing** Write a problem that can be solved using similar triangles. Draw a diagram and solve the problem.

19. **Open-Ended** Estimate your walking rate in feet per second. Write this rate in miles per hour.

20. **Reasoning** An item costs $64. The price is increased by 10%, then reduced by 10%. Is the final price equal to the original price? Explain.

Name _____ Class _____ Date _____

Chapter 2 Part A Test

Form K

Lessons 2-1 through 2-5

Do You Know HOW?

Solve each equation. Check your answer.

1. $9g + 12 = 84$

2. $\frac{1}{4}(z + 2) = \frac{3}{4}$

3. $n + 11.2 = 25.1$

4. $8x - 12 = 4x + 24$

5. $\frac{1}{5}(x - 8) = x - 16$

6. $\frac{x - 4}{6} = \frac{5}{4}$

Solve each equation. Justify your steps.

7. $8 + 6m = 26$

8. $-6 = \frac{1}{5}y - 1$

Solve each equation. If the equation is an identity, write *identity*. If it has no real-number solution, write *no solution*.

9. $\frac{1}{3}(6x - 12) = 4\left(\frac{1}{2}x + 1\right) - 2$

10. $\frac{p - 6}{2} = p - 4$

11. $2.6(t + 2) = 2(1.3t + 2) + 1.2$

12. $2x + 4 = 5(x + 1) - 3(x + 2)$

13. Jackie earns $172 per week at her part time job. She is saving this money to buy a used car that costs $2000. At this rate, how many weeks will it take her to earn enough money to buy the car?

Solve each equation for the given variable.

14. $-3b + ac = c - 4$ for c

15. $\frac{x}{y} + 4 = \frac{z}{5}$ for x

Chapter 2 Part A Test (continued)

Form K

Lessons 2-1 through 2-5

Define a variable and write an equation for each situation. Then solve.

16. A large cheese pizza costs $7.50. Each additional topping for the pizza costs $1.35. If the total bill for the pizza Sally ordered was $12.90, how many toppings did she order?

17. A water park offers a season pass for $64 per person which includes free admission and free parking. Admission for the water park is $14.50 per person. Parking is normally $5 for those without a season pass.
    a. How many visits to the water park would you have to use for the season pass to be a better deal?
    b. What would the total cost be for 3 visits with and without a season pass?

18. The length of a rectangle is twice the width. An equation that models the perimeter of the rectangle is $2w + 4w = 36$ where w is the width of the rectangle in ft. What are the length and the width of the rectangle?

19. Two consecutive odd integers can be modeled by n and $n + 2$, where n is an odd integer. The sum of two consecutive odd integers is 80. What are the integers?

Do You UNDERSTAND?

20. **Writing** Describe the steps that are involved in solving the equation $9 = 6 + \frac{z - 8}{4}$.

21. **Open-Ended** Write a multi-step equation for each condition listed below.

    a. equation has no solution

    b. equation has one solution

    c. equation is an identity

Chapter 2 Part B Test

Form K

Lessons 2-6 through 2-10

Do You Know HOW?

Convert the given amount to the given unit.

1. 8 ft; in.

2. 2.5 miles; ft

3. 260 sec; min

Solve each proportion. Use the Multiplication Property of Equality or the Cross Product Property. Explain your choice.

4. $\frac{1}{a} = \frac{6}{18}$

5. $\frac{x+1}{15} = \frac{-4}{5}$

6. $\frac{2}{q} = \frac{8}{q+12}$

Solve each proportion.

7. $\frac{2.5}{10} = \frac{m}{4}$

8. $\frac{14}{49} = \frac{4}{x}$

9. $\frac{k}{10} = \frac{9}{6}$

10. The figures at the right are similar. Find the missing length.

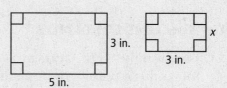

3 in.

x

3 in.

5 in.

11. What percent of 50 is 30?

12. What is 45% of 120?

Tell whether each percent change is an increase or decrease. Then find the percent change.

13. Original amount: $46
New amount: $52

14. Original amount: $25
New amount: $35

15. Original amount: $99.50
New amount: $92.50

16. Original amount: $19.25
New amount: $22.75

Chapter 2 Part B Test (continued)   *Form K*

Lessons 2-6 through 2-10

Define a variable and write an equation for each situation. Then solve.

17. There are 21 females in the Algebra 1 class. If 75% of the class is female, how many students are there in the class?

18. The scale of a map is 1 in. : 75 km. Determine the distance between two towns that are 5.6 in. apart on the map.

19. A flagpole casts a 32-ft shadow. A boy who is 6 feet tall is standing near the flagpole casting a 16-ft shadow. They form similar triangles. How tall is the flagpole?

20. In 2005, a car sold new for $12,500. In 2008, value of the car was $8750. Find the percent decrease.

Do You UNDERSTAND?

21. Error Analysis The average class grade went from 86% to an 81%. Susie thinks this represents a 5% change in the average. Explain Susie's error. What is the actual percent decrease?

22. Open-Ended Write a problem that can be solved using proportions. Write the proportion and solve the problem.

23. Writing Suppose you are given two similar triangles. All three side lengths of one triangle are given and one side length of the other triangle is given. Explain how you can find one of the missing side lengths. Include the steps for solving for the missing length.

Performance Tasks

Chapter 2

TASK 1

Suppose that you are the teacher. Look at the three equations below and provide a detailed description of how to solve each equation. Be sure to include in your discussion the different steps needed to solve each equation, and how the steps differ.

  a. $2x + 7 = 24$ **b.** $\dfrac{w}{4} - 2 = 12$ **c.** $\dfrac{5k + 3}{4} = -10$

  d. After you finish your discussion about the three equations above, you are anxious to show the class how these types of equations can model real-world situations. Write a description of two real-world situations: one that can be modeled by a one-step equation and one that can be modeled by a two-step equation. Write the equations and solve them.

TASK 2

The relationship between the temperature in degrees Fahrenheit, F, and the temperature in degrees Celsius, C, is represented by the formula $F = \dfrac{9}{5}C + 32$.

  a. Solve the formula for C to express the Celsius temperature in terms of the Fahrenheit temperature.

  b. A classmate tells you that there is one Fahrenheit temperature that is the same as the Celsius temperature. Is your classmate correct? If so, what is the temperature? If your classmate is incorrect, explain why.

Performance Tasks (continued)

Chapter 2

TASK 3

Solve one proportion using properties of equality. Solve the other using cross products. Explain the steps you used in each process.

  a. $\dfrac{x}{21} = \dfrac{4}{7}$ $\qquad\qquad\qquad\qquad$ $\dfrac{7}{4} = \dfrac{21}{x}$

  b. Create a proportion that models a real-world situation. Be sure to define the variable, relate it to a model, write the equation, and solve the proportion.

TASK 4

Michael has made a scale drawing of his classroom. The scale for his drawing is 0.5 in. : 3 ft.

  a. The length of the classroom is 30 ft. The length of the room on the scale drawing is 6 in. Is this correct? Explain why or why not.

  b. One of the student tables is 6 ft long. How long should it be on the drawing? Explain how you got your answer.

  c. Write your own problem concerning Michael's drawing. Solve and explain your answers.

Cumulative Review

Chapters 1-2

Multiple Choice

For Exercises 1–10, choose the correct letter.

1. Which algebraic expression represents 15 less than the product of 7 and a number?
   A. $15 - 7n$
   B. $7n - 15$
   C. $15(7n)$
   D. $7(n - 15)$

2. Which of the following is the correct simplification of $7 \cdot 4^2 \div 8 - 12$?
   F. -28
   G. $-\frac{17}{2}$
   H. -5
   I. 2

3. What is the value of $\dfrac{3m^2 - mn}{2mn^2}$ when $m = -1$ and $n = 2$?
   A. $-\frac{5}{8}$
   B. $-\frac{1}{8}$
   C. $\frac{1}{8}$
   D. $\frac{5}{8}$

4. What is the solution of $-6x + 15 = -3$?
   F. -3
   G. -2
   H. 3
   I. 6

5. What is the solution of $4x - 6 = -6x - 4$?
   A. $-\frac{3}{2}$
   B. -1
   C. $\frac{1}{5}$
   D. 1

6. What is the solution of $\frac{3}{5} = \frac{x}{15}$?
   F. 1
   G. 6
   H. 9
   I. 25

7. A scale drawing of a building has the scale 0.5 in. : 6 ft. A wall is 30 ft long. How long will the wall be on the drawing?
   A. 1.5 in.
   B. 2.5 in.
   C. 6 in.
   D. 360 in.

8. What is the simplified form of the expression $\sqrt{225}$?
   F. -25
   G. 15
   H. 20
   I. does not simplify

9. Which property is illustrated by $45 + 19 = 19 + 45$?
   A. Commutative Property of Addition
   B. Identity Property of Addition
   C. Associative Property of Addition
   D. Zero Property of Addition

10. What percent of 86 is 50 to the nearest whole percent?
    F. 43%
    G. 58%
    H. 59%
    I. 172%

Cumulative Review (continued)

Chapters 1-2

11. A store's cost for a stereo was $27. The markup was 75%. A customer purchased it on sale at 40% off the marked up price. What was the purchase price of the stereo?

12. Evaluate each expression for $x = 3$ and $y = 2$.

    a. $-4x + 3y$

    b. $\dfrac{x^2 - y}{4x}$

13. Find the percent of decrease for each situation.
    a. $250 is discounted to $212.50

    b. $40 is discounted to $32

14. The school choir has 84 members. The ratio of girls to boys in the choir is $3 : 4$. How many members are girls?

Find each answer.

15. Solve: $-2(3x + 2) = 2x + 6$

16. Simplify: $-\sqrt{169}$

17. Solve: $\dfrac{3}{4} = \dfrac{8}{x - 1}$

18. Simplify: $14 + 2 \times 8 - 5^2 + 3^2$

19. Solve: $6n - 7 = 35$

20. Solve: $\dfrac{x - 1}{2} = \dfrac{x + 3}{-1}$

21. The scale of a map is 0.25 cm : 15 mi. Determine the distance between two cities that are 6.8 cm apart on the map.

22. The price of the car was marked as $14,000. The end of the month sale has lowered the price to $12,500. What is the percent decrease to the nearest percent?

23. Four times the sum of a number and -3 is 4 more than twice the number. Write and solve an equation to find the number.

24. Jeremy is putting together a model rocket. The scale is 1 cm : 50 ft. If the height of the actual rocket is 210 feet, how tall is the model?

25. **Writing** Describe four different subsets of real numbers. Explain the differences between the various subsets. Give several examples of each subset.

Chapter 2 Project Teacher Notes: The Big Dig!

About the Project

The project gives students an opportunity to explore the mathematical connection between height and lengths of bones in the human body. The activities will help students understand how to measure and display data.

Introducing the Project

- Ask students to work with partners or in small groups. Students will need to know that the tibia is the inner and thicker of the two bones between the knee and the ankle, the humerus extends from the shoulder to the elbow, and the radius connects the wrist to the elbow.
- Discuss what tools and/or methods are available for measuring. Determine which would be best for this project and why. Discuss and evaluate ways to organize and display the data. Suggest that students create spreadsheets for calculating and displaying their information.

Activity 1: Graphing

Students list the lengths of the radius bones of all students and graph the data.

Activity 2: Calculating

Students calculate their own heights using the given formulas. Then they make suppositions about an archaeological find.

Activity 3: Analyzing

Students organize the data from Activity 1 by gender, then display the data to compare heights of males and females.

Activity 4: Creating

Students measure the tibia, humerus, and radius bones, and the heights of several adults. They organize their data on spreadsheets. Using the formulas from Activity 2, they predict heights and compare predictions with measured heights.

Finishing the Project

You may wish to plan a project day on which students share their completed projects. Encourage groups to explain their processes as well as their results. Have students review their project work and update their folders.

- Have students review their methods for finding, recording, and displaying the data they needed for the project.
- Ask groups to share insights that resulted from completing the project, such as any shortcuts they found for creating graphs and spreadsheets. Also, ask if any mathematical ideas have become more obvious, and whether there are areas about which they would like to learn more.

Chapter 2 Project: The Big Dig!

Beginning the Chapter Project

Your bones tell a lot about your body. Archaeologists and forensic scientists study bones to estimate a person's height, build, and age. These data are helpful in learning about ancient people and in solving crimes. The lengths of major bones, such as the humerus, radius, and tibia, can be substituted into formulas to estimate a person's height.

As you work through the activities, you will collect data from your classmates and from adults. You will use formulas to analyze the data and predict heights. Then you will decide how to organize and display your results in graphs and spreadsheets.

List of Materials
- Calculator
- Tape measure or ruler
- Graph paper

Activities

Activity 1: Graphing

In this activity, you will collect, graph, and analyze data.
- Measure the length of your radius bone to the nearest half inch.
- Collect the measurements taken by your classmates. (Note whether each measurement is that of a male or a female for Activity 3.) Display the data in a graph.
- Write a description of the data.

Activity 2: Calculating

Scientists use the formulas in the table at the right to approximate a person's height H, in inches, when they know the length of the tibia t, the humerus h, or the radius r.

- Use your tibia, humerus, and radius bone lengths to calculate your height. Are the calculated heights close to your actual height? Explain.
- An archaeologist found an 18-inch tibia on the site of an American colonial farm. Do you think it belonged to a man or woman? Why?
- Choose one radius measurement from the data you collected for Activity 1. Calculate the person's height. Can you tell whose height you have found? Explain.

Male
$H = 32.2 + 2.4t$
$H = 29.0 + 3.0h$
$H = 31.7 + 3.7r$

Female
$H = 28.6 + 2.5t$
$H = 25.6 + 3.1h$
$H = 28.9 + 3.9r$

Chapter 2 Project: The Big Dig! (continued)

Activity 3: Analyzing

When predicting height, scientists use different formulas for men and women.

- Review the data collected in Activity 1. Organize the data by male and female.
- Organize and display the data to see if there are differences between the heights of males and females.

Activity 4: Creating

In this activity, you will analyze data from adults.

- Measure the tibia, humerus, and radius bones, and the heights of several adults to the nearest half inch. Create a spreadsheet to organize the measurements. Use the formulas from Activity 2 in your spreadsheets to predict the heights of the adults.
- Compare the predicted heights with the measured heights. Does one of the formulas predict height better than the other formulas? Explain.

Finishing the Project

The answers to the four activities should help you complete your project. Assemble all the parts of your project in a folder. Include a summary of what you have learned about using the height formulas. What difficulties did you have? Are there ways to avoid these problems? What advice would you give to an archaeologist or forensic scientist about predicting heights from bone lengths?

Reflect and Revise

Ask a classmate to review your folder with you. Together, check that your graph is clearly labeled and accurate. Check that you have used formulas correctly and that your calculations are accurate. Is your spreadsheet well organized and easy to follow? Make any revisions necessary to improve your work.

Extending the Project

Archaeologists and forensic scientists use many other formulas related to the human body. Research formulas of this type by contacting your local police department or by searching the Internet.

Chapter 2 Project Manager: The Big Dig!

Getting Started

Read the project. As you work on the project, you will need a calculator, a tape measure or ruler, and materials to make accurate and attractive graphs. Keep all of your work for the project in a folder.

Checklist	Suggestions
☐ Activity 1: organizing and analyzing data	☐ Measure from the base of your thumb to the bend in your arm.
☐ Activity 2: using formulas	☐ Use the correct formulas for calculating your height. Try all three formulas to find the most accurate.
☐ Activity 3: comparing male and female data	☐ Choose an effective table or graph.
☐ Activity 4: comparing measurements	☐ Include data from family members, teachers, or neighbors.
☐ project display	☐ Why might the measurements taken by another group differ? How accurate are these data? Do your graphs and spreadsheet(s) support your predictions?

Scoring Rubric

4 Appropriate types of graphs and charts are chosen. Graphs are labeled correctly and completely, and show accurate scales. Formulas and calculations are accurate. The spreadsheet presents data clearly and is easy to follow. Explanations are clear and correct.

3 The spreadsheet is complete and clear. The graph and formulas are appropriately chosen and used. There are minor errors in scale or computation. Reasoning and explanations are essentially correct, but sometimes awkward or unclear.

2 Graphs and selected formulas are somewhat correct. Calculations contain many errors. Explanations are not adequate.

1 Major elements of the project are incomplete or missing.

0 Project is not handed in or shows no effort.

Your Evaluation of Project Evaluate your work, based on the *Scoring Rubric*.

Teacher's Evaluation of Project

Page 1

2-1 ELL Support
Solving One-Step Equations

Two numbers with a sum equal to zero

□□□ + ■■■ = 0

3 + (−3) = 0

Opposites are additive inverses.

Sample 12 and −12 are additive inverses.

Solve.

1. $-32 + 32 =$ $\boxed{0}$

2. Circle the *additive inverse* of 6. $\boxed{-6}$ $-\frac{1}{6}$ $\frac{1}{6}$ 6

3. Circle the *additive inverse* of −18. −18 $-\frac{1}{18}$ $\frac{1}{18}$ $\boxed{18}$

4. Circle the *opposite* of 91. $\boxed{-91}$ $-\frac{1}{91}$ $\frac{1}{91}$ 91

5. Cross out the pairs of numbers that are NOT *additive inverses*.

27 and −27   4 and −4   ~~10 and 12~~ $\frac{2}{7}$ and $-\frac{2}{7}$ ~~15 and 11~~

Two numbers with a product equal to zero

$4 \times \frac{1}{4} = 1$ $4 \times 0.25 = 1$

Reciprocals are multiplicative inverses.

Sample 4 and $\frac{1}{4}$ are multiplicative inverses.

Solve.

6. $\frac{3}{7} \times \frac{7}{3} =$ $\boxed{1}$

7. Cross out the pairs of numbers that are NOT *multiplicative inverses*.

$\frac{3}{4}$ and $\frac{4}{3}$ ~~$\frac{4}{7}$ and 47~~ $\frac{9}{5}$ and $\frac{5}{9}$ 6 and $\frac{1}{6}$ 0.1 and 10

8. Circle the *multiplicative inverse* of 6. −6 $-\frac{1}{6}$ $\boxed{\frac{1}{6}}$ 6

9. Circle the *reciprocal* of −18. −18 $\boxed{-\frac{1}{18}}$ $\frac{1}{18}$ 188

Page 2

2-1 Think About a Plan
Solving One-Step Equations

Volleyball In volleyball, players serve the ball to the opposing team. If the opposing team fails to hit the ball, the service is called an ace. A player's ace average is the number of aces served divided by the number of games played. A certain player has an ace average of 0.3 and has played in 70 games this season. How many aces has the player served?

Understanding the Problem

1. What values are you given?
a player's ace average, 0.3, and the number of games the player played, 70

Planning the Solution

2. Write an expression, using words, to represent the relationship between ace average, number of aces, and the number of games played.

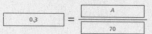

Ace Average = $\dfrac{\text{number of aces served}}{\text{number of games played}}$

3. Use the expression to write an equation, where A = number of aces.

$0.3 = \dfrac{A}{70}$

Getting an Answer

4. Solve the equation you wrote in Step 3.
21

5. Explain what this solution represents.
the number of aces served

6. Is your answer reasonable? Explain.
yes; $\frac{21}{70}$ is a little less than $\frac{1}{3}$ or about 0.3

Page 3

2-1 Practice   Form G
Solving One-Step Equations

Solve each equation using addition or subtraction. Check your answer.

1. $8 = a - 2$ 10

2. $x + 7 = 11$ 4

3. $r - 2 = -6$ −4

4. $-18 = m + 12$ −30

5. $f + 10 = -10$ −20

6. $-1 = n + 5$ −6

Solve each equation using multiplication or division. Check your answer.

7. $-3p = -48$ 16

8. $-98 = 7t$ −14

9. $-4.4 = -4y$ 1.1

10. $2.8c = 4.2$ 1.5

11. $\frac{k}{6} = 8$ 48

12. $16 = \frac{w}{8}$ 128

13. $-9 = \frac{y}{-3}$ 27

14. $\frac{h}{10} = \frac{-22}{5}$ −44

Solve each equation. Check your answer.

15. $\frac{3}{5}n = 12$ 20

16. $-4 = \frac{2}{3}b$ −6

17. $\frac{5}{8}x = -15$ −24

18. $\frac{1}{4}z = \frac{2}{5}$ $\frac{8}{5}$

19. Jeremy mowed several lawns to earn money for camp. After he paid $17 for gas, he had $75 leftover to pay towards camp. Write and solve an equation to find how much money Jeremy earned mowing lawns. $m - 17 = 75$; $92

Page 4

2-1 Practice (continued)   Form G
Solving One-Step Equations

Define a variable and write an equation for each situation. Then solve.

20. Susan's cell phone plan allows her to use 950 minutes per month with no additional charge. She has 188 minutes left for this month. How many minutes has she already used this month? $n + 188 = 950$; 762 minutes

21. In the fifth year of operation, the profit of a company was 3 times the profit it earned in the first year of operation. If its profit was $114,000 in the fifth year of operation, what was the profit in the first year? $3p = 114{,}000$; $38,000

Solve each equation. Check your answer.

22. $-9x = 48$ $-5\frac{1}{3}$

23. $-\frac{7}{8} = \frac{2}{3} + n$ $-\frac{37}{24}$

24. $a + 1\frac{1}{4} = 2\frac{7}{10}$ $1\frac{9}{20}$

25. $-7t = 5.6$ −0.8

26. $2.3 = -7.9 + y$ 10.2

27. $\frac{5}{3}p = \frac{8}{3}$ $\frac{8}{5}$

28. $\frac{g}{8} = -\frac{3}{4}$ −6

29. $\frac{m}{8} = 8\frac{1}{3}$ $66\frac{2}{3}$

30. A community center is serving a free meal to senior citizens. The center plans to feed 700 people in 4 hours.
a. Write and solve an equation to find the average number of people the center is planning to feed each hour. $4a = 700$; 175

b. During the first hour and a half, the center fed 270 people. Write and solve an equation to find the number of people that remain to be fed. $700 = n + 270$; 430 people

Page 5

2-1 Practice — Form K
Solving One-Step Equations

Solve each equation using addition or subtraction. Check your answer.

1. $6 = p - 8$ 14
2. $z + 5 = 4$ −1
3. $m - 4 = 12$ 16
4. $-10 = h - 4$ −6
5. $n + 14 = -5$ 19
6. $2 = a + 7$ −5

Solve each equation using multiplication or division. Check your answer.

7. $4t = -32$ −8
8. $-25 = -5x$ 5
9. $-3.2k = 16$ −5
10. $2.8r = 16.8$ 6
11. $\frac{m}{7} = 4$ 28
12. $25 = \frac{z}{-4}$ −100

Solve each equation. Check your answer.

13. $\frac{3}{4}b = 15$ 20
14. $-8 = \frac{2}{5}t$ −20
15. $\frac{9}{10}y = -36$ −40
16. $\frac{1}{2}m = \frac{6}{11}$ $\frac{12}{11}$

Page 6

2-1 Practice (continued) — Form K
Solving One-Step Equations

Define a variable and write an equation for each situation. Then solve.

17. Bradley has a goal to work 28 hours each week at the pizza shop. So far he has worked 12 hours. How many more hours does he need to work to meet his goal?
$h + 12 = 28$; 16 hrs

18. Sheree is 4 times as old as Benjamin. If Sheree is 72 years old, how old is Benjamin? $4B = 72$; 18 years old

Solve each equation. Check your answer.

19. $-8h = 26$ $-3\frac{1}{4}$
20. $-\frac{3}{5} = \frac{1}{10} + q$ $-\frac{7}{10}$
21. $n + 3\frac{2}{3} = 5\frac{7}{9}$ $2\frac{1}{9}$
22. $-9w = 6.3$ −0.7
23. $5.8 = -4.5 + z$ −10.3
24. $\frac{d}{5} = -\frac{3}{10}$ $-\frac{3}{2}$

25. A youth club is taking a field trip to a community farm. 27 members attended the trip. The total cost for the club was $148.50.
a. Write and solve an equation to determine the cost for each person.
$27x = 148.50$; $5.50
b. The farm brought in $1512.50 that day including what they received from the youth club. Write and solve an equation to find the number of people that visited the community farm that day. $5.50p = 1512.5$; 275 people

Page 7

2-1 Standardized Test Prep
Solving One-Step Equations

Multiple Choice

For Exercises 1–6, choose the correct letter.

1. What is the solution of $-3 = x + 5$? B
A. −15 B. −8 C. 2 D. 8

2. What operation should you use to solve $-6x = -24$? I
F. addition G. subtraction H. multiplication I. division

3. Which of the following solutions is true for $\frac{x}{3} = \frac{1}{4}$? C
A. $-2\frac{3}{4}$ B. $\frac{1}{12}$ C. $\frac{3}{4}$ D. $3\frac{1}{4}$

4. There are 37 more cats c than dogs d in an animal shelter. If there are 78 cats at the shelter, which equation represents the relationship between the number of cats and dogs? F
F. $d + 37 = 78$ G. $d - 37 = 78$ H. $c + 37 = 78$ I. $c - 37 = 78$

5. Which property of equality should you use to solve $6x = 48$? D
A. Addition Property of Equality
B. Subtraction Property of Equality
C. Multiplication Property of Equality
D. Division Property of Equality

6. Shelly completed 10 problems of her homework in study hall. This is $\frac{2}{5}$ of the total assignment. How many problems does she have left to complete? G
F. 20 G. 25 H. 30 I. 35

Short Response

7. A high school marching band has 55 male members. It is determined that five-eighths of the band members are male.
a. What equation represents the total number of members in the band? $\frac{5}{8}n = 55$;
b. How many members are in the band? 88 band members
[2] Both parts answered correctly.
[1] One part answered correctly.
[0] Neither part answered correctly.

Page 8

2-1 Enrichment
Solving One-Step Equations

Equivalent equations are equations that have the same solution(s). For example, the equations $\frac{x}{3} = 6$ and $x - 6 = 12$ are equivalent because the solution of each is $x = 18$. Every equation has many equivalent equations.

There are four different forms of equations representing the four different operations mentioned in the lesson. If a and b represent constants, the different forms can be represented by the following equations:

1) $x + a = b$ 　　2) $ax = b$
3) $x - a = b$ 　　4) $\frac{x}{a} = b$

Determine which equations in the following exercises are equivalent. If they are equivalent, justify your answer. If not, explain.

1. $-2x = 14$ 　$-x - 8 = -15$ 　$\frac{x}{7} = -1$ 　$-19 = x - 12$
all equations are equivalent; for all, $x = -7$

2. $y - 8 = 12$ 　$\frac{y}{2} = 2$ 　$2y = 40$ 　$-22 = y - 42$
first, third, and fouth equations are equivalent; $y = 20$ except for the second equation where $y = 4$

3. $-6n = -12$ 　$n + 8 = 6$ 　$-4 = n - 2$ 　$\frac{n}{2} = 1$
first and fourth equations are equivalent ($n = 2$); second and third equations are equivalent ($n = -2$);

For each of the following equations, find three equivalent equations in the three other forms that are different from the original equation. For example, $x + 3 = 5$, $3x = 6$, and $\frac{x}{2} = 1$ are equivalent because $x = 2$ is the solution of each equation.

4. $x + 6 = -5$
Answers may vary. Sample: The solution of the given equation is $x = -11$, so $20 + x = 9$, $3x = -33$, and $x + 2 = -9$ are equivalent.

5. $8x = -24$
Answers may vary. Sample: The solution of $8x = -24$, is −3, so $10 + x = 7$, $15 - x = 18$, and $5x = -15$ are equivalent.

6. $\frac{x}{3} = -9$
Answers may vary. Sample: The solution $\frac{x}{3} = -9$ is −27, so $x + 30 = 3$, $4x = -108$, and $x - 6 = -33$ are equivalent.

7. $14 = x - 18$
Answers may vary. Sample: The solution of $14 = x - 18$, is 32. So, $x - 10 = 22$, $\frac{x}{8} = 4$, and $x + 15 = 47$ are equivalent.

Page 9

2-1 Reteaching
Solving One-Step Equations

You can use the properties of equality to solve equations. Subtraction is the inverse of addition.

Problem

What is the solution of $x + 5 = 33$?

In the equation, $x + 5 = 33$, 5 is added to the variable. To solve the equation, you need to isolate the variable, or get it alone on one side of the equal sign. Undo adding 5 by subtracting 5 from each side of the equation.

Drawing a diagram can help you write an equation to solve the problem.

Whole		33	
Part	Part	x	5

Solve
$$x + 5 = 33$$
$$x + 5 - 5 = 33 - 5 \qquad \text{Undo adding 5 by subtracting 5.}$$
$$x = 28 \qquad \text{Simplify. This isolates } x.$$

Check
$$x + 5 = 33 \qquad \text{Check your solution in the original equation.}$$
$$28 + 5 \overset{?}{=} 33 \qquad \text{Substitute 28 for } x.$$
$$33 = 33 \checkmark$$

The solution to $x + 5 = 33$ is 28.

Division is the inverse of multiplication.

Problem

What is the solution of $\frac{x}{5} = 12$?

In the equation, $\frac{x}{5} = 12$, the variable is divided by 5. Undo dividing by 5 by multiplying by 5 on each side of the equation.

	x			
12	12	12	12	12

Solve
$$\frac{x}{5} = 12$$
$$\frac{x}{5} \cdot 5 = 12 \cdot 5 \qquad \text{Undo dividing by 5 by multiplying by 5.}$$
$$x = 60 \qquad \text{Simplify. This isolates } x.$$

The solution to $\frac{x}{5} = 12$ is 60.

Page 10

2-1 Reteaching (continued)
Solving One-Step Equations

Exercises

Solve each equation using addition or subtraction. Check your answer.

1. $-3 = n + 9$ -12

2. $f + 6 = -6$ -12

3. $m + 12 = 22$ 10

4. $r + 2 = 7$ 5

5. $b + 1.1 = -11$ -12.1

6. $t + 9 = 4$ -5

Define a variable and write an equation for each situation. Then solve.

7. A student is taking a test. He has 37 questions left. If the test has 78 questions, how many questions has he finished? $f + 37 = 78$; 41

8. A friend bought a bouquet of flowers. The bouquet had nine daisies and some roses. There were a total of 15 flowers in the bouquet. How many roses were in the bouquet? $9 + r = 15$; 6

Solve each equation using multiplication or division. Check your answer.

9. $\frac{z}{8} = 2$ 16

10. $-26 = \frac{c}{13}$ -338

11. $\frac{q}{11} = -6$ -66

12. $-\frac{a}{3} = 18$ -54

13. $-25 = \frac{g}{5}$ -125

14. $20.4 = \frac{s}{2.5}$ 51

15. A student has been typing for 22 minutes and has typed a total of 1496 words. Write and solve an equation to determine the average number of words she can type per minute. $22a = 1496$; 68

Page 11

2-2 ELL Support
Solving Two-Step Equations

Use the chart below to review vocabulary. These vocabulary words will help you complete this page.

Related Words	Explanations	Examples
solution suh 'loo shun	The value that makes an equation true A method for answering a problem	A solution to $x + 2 = 5$ is 3 because $3 + 2 = 5$.
solve sahlv	To work out a correct answer to a problem	She was able to solve the hardest problem on the test.
solving SAHL ving	Finding an answer to a problem	He spent an hour solving his homework problems.

Use the vocabulary above to fill in the blanks. The first one is done for you.

The teacher wants all her students to get the correct __solution__ to the problem on the test.

1. The purpose of the test was to __solve__ ten problems.

2. __Solving__ the easiest problem only took a minute.

Circle the correct answer.

3. What is the solution of the equation $2x - 35 = 15$?   10   15   20   (25)

4. Which answer solves the equation $5y + 25 = 50$?   (5)   10   25   50

Fill-in-the-blank

A package of flashcards tests addition, subtraction, multiplication, and division. There are 12 cards for each operation. Derek found a deck that has 46 cards. How many cards are missing from the deck?

Know
5. There are ⟦12⟧ cards for each operation.

6. There are ⟦4⟧ operations in a deck of flash cards.

7. How many cards did Derek find? ⟦46⟧

Need
8. How many cards are in a full deck? ⟦12⟧ × ⟦4⟧ = ⟦48⟧

Plan
9. To find the number of missing cards, you will need to __subtract the__ number of cards Derek found from the number of cards in a full deck.

Page 12

2-2 Think About a Plan
Solving Two-Step Equations

Earth Science The temperature beneath Earth's surface increases by 10°C per kilometer. The surface temperature and the temperature at the bottom of a mine are shown. How many kilometers below Earth's surface is the bottom of the mine?

Surface: 18°C

Bottom of mine: 38°C

Understanding the Problem

1. What happens to the temperature as the distance below Earth's surface increases?
   The temperature increases 10°C per km.

2. What do you need to determine?
   how far below Earth's surface the mine is

3. What is the change in temperature from Earth's surface to the bottom of the mine?
   The temperature increases 20°C.

Planning the Solution

4. Write an expression for how much the temperature increases x kilometers below the surface.
   $10x$

5. Write an equation that relates the change in temperature, from 18°C at Earth's surface to 38°C at the bottom of the mine, to the expression for how much the temperature increases x kilometers below the surface.
   $38 - 18 = 10x$

Getting an Answer

6. Solve the equation.
   $x = 2$

7. Is your answer reasonable? Explain.
   yes; an increase of 20°C

Page 13

2-2 **Practice** Form G
Solving Two-Step Equations

Solve each equation. Check your answer.

1. $6 + 3b = -18$ -8

2. $-3 + 5x = 12$ 3

3. $7n + 12 = -23$ -5

4. $\frac{t}{6} - 3 = 8$ 66

5. $-12 = 8 + \frac{f}{2}$ -40

6. $13 = 8 - 5d$ -1

7. $\frac{k}{4} + 6 = -2$ -32

8. $-22 = -8 + 7y$ -2

9. $16 - 3p = 34$ -6

10. $15 + \frac{q}{6} = -21$ -216

11. $-19 + \frac{c}{3} = 8$ 81

12. $-18 - 11r = 26$ -4

13. $-9 = \frac{y}{-3} - 6$ 9

14. $14 + \frac{m}{10} = 24$ 100

Define a variable and write an equation for each situation. Then solve.

15. Chip earns a base salary of $500 per month as a salesman. In addition to the salary, he earns $90 per product that he sells. If his goal is to earn $5000 per month, how many products does he need to sell?
$500 + 90n = 5000$; 50 products

16. A pizza shop charges $9 for a large cheese pizza. Additional toppings cost $1.25 per topping. Heather paid $15.25 for her large pizza. How many toppings did she order?
$9 + 1.25n = 15.25$; 5 toppings

Page 14

2-2 **Practice** (continued) Form G
Solving Two-Step Equations

Solve each equation. Check your answer.

17. $\frac{z + 6}{3} = 8$ 18

18. $\frac{n - 7}{2} = -11$ -15

19. $\frac{j + 18}{-4} = 8$ -50

20. $\frac{1}{3}a - 6 = -15$ -27

21. $\frac{1}{4} = \frac{1}{4}h + 4$ -15

22. $6.42 - 10d = 2.5$ 0.392

23. The selling price of a television in a retail store is $66 less than 3 times the wholesale price. If the selling price of a television is $899, write and solve an equation to find the wholesale price of the television.
$3w - 66 = 899$; $321.67

24. The fare for a taxicab is $5 per trip plus $0.50 per mile. The fare for the trip from the airport to the convention center was $11.50. Write and solve an equation to find how many miles the trip is from the airport to the convention center.
$5 + 0.50m = 11.50$; 13 miles

25. An online movie club offers a membership for $5 per month. Members can rent movies for $1.50 per rental. A member was billed $15.50 one month. Write and solve an equation to find how many movies the member rented.
$5 + 1.50n = 15.50$; 7 movies

26. **Writing** Describe, using words, how to solve the equation $6 - 4x = 18$. List any properties utilized in the solution.

$6 - 4x = 18$
$6 - 6 - 4x = 18 - 6$ Subtract 6 from both sides. (Subt. Prop. of Equal.)
$-4x = 12$ Simplify.
$\frac{-4x}{-4} = \frac{12}{-4}$ Divide both sides by -4. (Div. Prop. of Equal.)
$x = -3$ Simplify.

27. **a.** Solve $-8 = \frac{x + 2}{4}$ -34

b. Write the right side of the equation in part (a) as the sum of two fractions. Solve the equation. -34

c. Did you find the equation in part (a) or the rewritten equation easier to solve? Why? Answers may vary. Sample: the original equation; It's easier to subtract whole numbers than a whole number and a fraction.

Page 15

2-2 **Practice** Form K
Solving Two-Step Equations

Solve each equation. Check your answer.

1. $4x + 5 = 13$ 2

2. $-8 + 3h = 1$ 3

3. $2j - 13 = 25$ 19

4. $\frac{n}{5} - 1 = 7$ 40

5. $-5 = -8 + \frac{y}{10}$ 30

6. $7 = -6m + 7$ 0

7. $\frac{n}{-8} - 5 = -2$ -24

8. $-14 = -6 + 4w$ -2

9. $15 - 3t = -12$ 9

10. $13 + \frac{a}{11} = 7$ -66

Define a variable and write an equation for each situation. Then solve.

11. A fair charges $7.25 for admission and $5.50 for a ride pass. Ten friends visited the fair. Not all of the friends purchased ride passes. If their total cost was $105.50, how many friends purchased ride passes?
Let r represent the ride passes; $72.50 + 5.50r = 105.50$; 6 ride passes

12. A cafeteria sells entrées and additional items. An entrée costs $4.75, and each additional item costs $1.25. A customer pays $9.75 for one entree and some additional items. How many additional items were ordered?
Let a represent the additional items; $4.75 + 1.25a = 9.75$; 4 items

Page 16

2-2 **Practice** (continued) Form K
Solving Two-Step Equations

Solve each equation. Check your answer.

13. $\frac{f + 4}{2} = 5$ 6

14. $\frac{p - 6}{3} = -15$ -39

15. $\frac{c + 5}{-6} = -4$ 19

16. $\frac{1}{4}z + 9 = -1$ -40

17. $\frac{1}{2} = \frac{1}{2}t + 3$ -5

18. $4.52 - 5h = 2.8$ 0.344

19. Jasmine is 23 years old. Jasmine is 3 years less than half of George's age. Write and solve an equation to find George's age.
$\frac{1}{2}G - 3 = 23$; 52 years old

20. An appliance repair person charges $55 per trip plus $15 per hour for her labor. The cost of fixing a stove was $92.50. Write and solve an equation to find how many hours it took to repair the stove.
$55 + 15h = 92.50$; 2.5 hrs

21. Shelly has a cell phone plan that costs $9.99 per month plus $0.05 per minute. Her total bill for the month is $25.59. Write and solve an equation to find how many minutes she used for the month.
$9.99 + 0.05m = 25.59$; 312 minutes

22. **Writing** Describe using words how to solve the equation $3 - 5n = -22$. Describe the properties utilized in the solution.
Sample: Use the subtraction property of equality to subtract 3 from both sides. The equation becomes $-5n = -25$. Use the division property of equality to divide each side by -5. The solution is 5.

Page 17

2-2 Standardized Test Prep
Solving Two-Step Equations

Gridded Response

Solve each exercise and enter your answer on the grid provided.

1. What is the solution of $-28 = 22 - 5x$? 10

2. What is the solution of $\frac{m}{4} - 3 = 7$? 40

3. The amount of money that Pamela p has and Julie j has are related by the equation $3p + 5 = j$. If Julie has $83, how much money does Pamela have? $26

4. An ice cream sundae costs $1.75 plus an additional $0.35 for each topping. If the total cost is $2.80, how many toppings did the sundae have? 3

5. The cost of a gallon of gasoline g is $3.25 less than 2 times the cost of a gallon of diesel d. If a gallon of gasoline costs $3.95, what is the cost of a gallon of diesel? $3.60

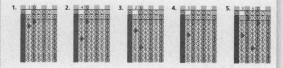

Page 18

2-2 Enrichment
Solving Two-Step Equations

Equations are used in geometry. One example is the relationship between the angles that are formed by intersecting lines. The measures of the pairs of opposite angles are equal. The measures of two adjacent angles add up to 180°.

Use the drawing shown to answer the following questions.

1. $m\angle 1 = 30$ and $m\angle 2 = 4x$. What is the value of x? 37.5

2. $m\angle 3 = 5x$ and $m\angle 4 = 75$. What is the value of x? 21

3. $m\angle 4 = 45$ and $m\angle 2 = 9x$. What is the value of x? 5

The formula for the perimeter of a rectangle is $P = 2l + 2w$, where l is the length and w is the width of the rectangle.

4. The width of a rectangle is 12 ft. The perimeter of the rectangle is 42 ft. What is the length of the rectangle? 9 ft

5. The perimeter of a rectangle is 158.5 cm. The length of the rectangle is 42.5 cm. What is the width of the rectangle? 36.75 cm

Another geometric application for 2-step equations involves the measures of the interior angles of a polygon. Regardless of the number of sides, n, a polygon has, the sum of the measures of the interior angles is $180n - 360$ degrees.

For example, the sum of the measures of the angles of a rectangle is $180(4) - 360 = 360°$.

The sum of the measures of the interior angles of various polygons are given. Set up an equation and solve to find the number of sides of each polygon.

6. 1080° 8 sides
7. 1440° 10 sides
8. 2340° 15 sides
9. 180° 3 sides
10. 3600° 22 sides
11. 540° 5 sides

Page 19

2-2 Reteaching
Solving Two-Step Equations

Properties of equality and inverse operations can be used to solve equations that involve more than one step to solve. To solve a two-step equation, identify the operations and undo them using inverse operations. Undo the operations in the reverse order of the order of operations.

Problem

What is the solution of $5x - 8 = 32$?

$5x - 8 + 8 = 32 + 8$ To get the variable term alone on the left side, add 8 to each side.

$5x = 40$ Simplify.

$\frac{5x}{5} = \frac{40}{5}$ Divide each side by 5 since x is being multiplied by 5 on the left side. This isolates x.

$x = 8$ Simplify.

Check $5x - 8 = 32$ Check your solution in the original equation.

$5(8) - 8 = 32$ Substitute 8 for x.

$32 = 32 ✓$ Simplify.

To solve $-16 = \frac{x}{3} + 5$, you can use subtraction first to undo the addition, and then use multiplication to undo the division.

Problem

What is the solution of $-16 = \frac{x}{3} + 5$?

$-16 - 5 = \frac{x}{3} + 5 - 5$ To get the variable term alone on the right, subtract 5 from each side.

$-21 = \frac{x}{3}$ Simplify.

$3(-21) = 3\left(\frac{x}{3}\right)$ Since x is being divided by 3, multiply each side by 3 to undo the division. This isolates x.

$-63 = x$ Simplify.

Page 20

2-2 Reteaching (continued)
Solving Two-Step Equations

Solve each equation. Check your answer.

1. $4f - 8 = 20$ 7
2. $25 - 6b = 55$ -5
3. $-z + 7 = -8$ 15
4. $\frac{w}{-9} + 7 = 10$ -27
5. $25 = 8 + \frac{n}{2}$ 34
6. $\frac{y - 8}{3} = -7$ -13

Solve each equation. Justify each step.

7. $6d - 5 = 31$ $6d - 5 + 5 = 31 + 5$ Add 5 to each side. (Add. Prop. of Equal.)

$6d = 36$ Simplify.

$\frac{6d}{6} = \frac{36}{6}$ Divide both sides by 6. (Div. Prop. of Equal.)

$d = 6$ Simplify.

8. $\frac{p - 7}{-2} = 5$ $-2 \cdot \frac{p - 7}{-2} = 5 \cdot -2$ Add 6 to both sides (Add. Prop. of Equal.)

$p - 7 = -10$ Simplify.

$p - 7 + 7 = -10 + 7$ Multiply both sides by 3. (Mult. Prop. of Equal.)

$p = -3$ Simplify.

Define a variable and write an equation for each situation. Then solve.

9. Ray's birthday is 8 more than four times the number of days away from today than Jane's birthday. If Ray's birthday is 24 days from today, how many days until Jane's birthday? $24 = 8 + 4j$; in 4 days

10. Jerud weighs 15 pounds less than twice Kate's weight. How much does Kate weigh if Jerud weighs 205 pounds? $205 = 2k - 15$; 110 lb

11. A phone company charges a flat fee of $17 per month, which includes free local calling plus $0.08 per minute for long distance calls. The Taylor's phone bill for the month is $31.80. How many minutes of long distance calling did they use during the month? $17 - 0.08m = 31.80$; 185 min

12. A delivery company charges a flat rate of $3 for a large envelope plus an additional $0.25 per ounce for every ounce over a pound the package weighs. The postage for the package is $5.50. How much does the package weigh? (Hint: remember the first pound is included in the $3.) $5.50 = 3 + 0.25c$; 1 lb 10 oz;

Page 21

2-3 ELL Support
Solving Multi-Step Equations

Problem

What is the solution of the multi-step equation $3x + 7 + 6x = 34$? Justify your steps. Then check your solution.

$3x + 7 + 6x = 34$	Write the original equation.
$3x + 6x + 7 = 34$	Commutative Property of Addition
$9x + 7 = 34$	Combine like terms.
$9x + \boxed{7 - 7} = 34 - 7$	Subtract 7 from each side. Subtraction Property of Equality
$9x = 27$	Simplify.
$\frac{9x}{9} = \frac{27}{9}$	Divide each side by 9. Division Property of Equality
$x = 3$	Simplify.

Check

$3x + 7 + 6x = 34$	Copy the original equation.
$3(3) + 7 + 6(3) = 34$	Substitute 3 for x.
$9 + 7 + 18 = 34$	Simplify.
$34 = 34$ ✓	

Exercise

What is the solution to the multi-step equation $4d - 2 + 3d = 61$? Justify your steps. Then check your solution.

$4d - 2 + 3d = 61$	Write the original equation.
$4d + 3d - 2 = 61$	Commutative Property of Addition
$7d - 2 = 61$	Combine like terms.
$7d - 2 + 2 = 61 + 2$	Add 2 to each side. Addition Property of Equality
$7d = 63$	Simplify.
$\frac{7d}{7} = \frac{63}{7}$	Divide each side by 7. Division Property of Equality
$d = 9$	Simplify.

Check

$4d - 2 + 3d = 61$	Copy the original equation.
$4(9) - 2 + 3(9) = 61$	Substitute $\underline{9}$ for d.
$\boxed{36} - 2 + \boxed{27} = 61$	Simplify.
$\boxed{61} = 61$ ✓	

Page 22

2-3 Think About a Plan
Solving Multi-Step Equations

Online Video Games Angie and Kenny play online video games. Angie buys 1 software package and 3 months of game play. Kenny buys 1 software package and 2 months of game play. Each software package costs $20. If their total cost is $115, what is the cost of one month of game play?

Know

1. What values are you given?
the number of software packages Angie and Kenny buy, the number of months they play, the cost of one software package, the total cost

Need

2. What do you need to find?
the cost of one month of play

Plan

3. What equation can you use to solve the problem?
$20 + 3c + 20 + 2c = 115$

4. Solve the equation. Show your work and justify each step.

$20 + 20 + 3c + 2c = 115$	Comm. Prop. of Add.
$40 + 5c = 115$	Combine like terms.
$40 - 40 + 5c = 115 - 40$	Subtract 40 from each side. (Subt. Prop. of Equal.)
$5c = 75$	Simplify.
$\frac{5c}{5} = 75$	Divide both sides by 5. (Div. Prop. of Equal.)
$c = 15$	Simplify.

5. Check your answer.
$20 + 3(15) + 20 + 2(15) \stackrel{?}{=} 115$
$20 + 45 + 20 + 30 \stackrel{?}{=} 115$
$115 = 115$ ✓

6. Is your answer reasonable? Explain.
yes; 5 months of play accounts for $75 of the total cost, so $15 is reasonable

Page 23

2-3 Practice — Form G
Solving Multi-Step Equations

Solve each equation. Check your answer.

1. $19 - h - h = -13$
16

2. $14 + 6a - 8 = 18$
2

3. $25 = 7 + 3k - 12$
10

4. $5n - 16 - 8n = -10$
−2

5. $-34 = v + 42 - 5v$
19

6. $x - 1 + 5x = 23$
4

7. $42j + 18 - 19j = -28$
−2

8. $-49 = 6c - 13 - 4c$
−18

9. $-28 + 15 - 22z = 31$
−2

Write an equation to model each situation. Then solve the equation.

10. General admission tickets to the fair cost $3.50 per person. Ride passes cost an additional $5.50 per person. Parking costs $6 for the family. The total costs for ride passes and parking was $51. How many people in the family attended the fair? $3.50p + 5.50p + 6 = 51$; 5 people

11. Five times a number decreased by 18 minus 4 times the same number is −36. What is the number? $5n - 18 - 4n = -36$; −18

Solve each equation. Check your answer.

12. $6(3m + 5) = 66$
2

13. $3(4y - 8) = 12$
3

14. $-5(x - 3) = -25$
8

15. $42 = 3(2 - 3h)$
−4

16. $-10 = 5(2w - 4)$
1

17. $(3p - 4) = 31$
$11\frac{2}{3}$

18. $-3 = -3(2t - 1)$
1

19. $x - 2(x + 10) = 12$
−32

20. $-15 = 5(3q - 10) - 5q$
3.5

21. Angela ate at the same restaurant four times. Each time she ordered a salad and left a $5 tip. She spent a total of $54. Write and solve an equation to find the cost of each salad. $4c + 4 \times 5 = 54$; $8.50

Page 24

2-3 Practice (continued) — Form G
Solving Multi-Step Equations

Solve each equation. Choose the method you prefer to use. Check your answer.

22. $\frac{a}{7} + \frac{5}{7} = \frac{2}{7}$
−3

23. $6v - \frac{5}{8} = \frac{7}{8}$
$\frac{1}{4}$

24. $\frac{j}{6} - 9 = \frac{5}{6}$
59

25. $\frac{x}{5} - \frac{1}{2} = \frac{3}{4}$
$3\frac{3}{4}$

26. $\frac{8}{9} + \frac{5}{6} = 6$
$25\frac{5}{6}$

27. $\frac{b}{9} - \frac{1}{2} = \frac{5}{18}$
7

28. $0.52y + 2.5 = 5.1$
5

29. $4n + 0.24 = 15.76$
3.88

30. $2.45 - 3.1t = 21.05$
−6

31. $-4.2 = 9.1x + 23.1$
−3

32. $11.3 - 7.2f = -3.82$
2.1

33. $14.2 = -6.8 + 4.2d$
5

34. **Reasoning** Suppose you want to solve $-5 = 6x + 3 + 7x$. What would you do as your first step? Explain.
Combine the like terms 6x and 7x by first grouping them and then adding their coefficients.

35. **Writing** Describe two different ways to solve $-10 = \frac{1}{4}(8y - 12)$.
Multiply both sides of the equation by 4 or distribute the $\frac{1}{4}$. Then isolate the variable using the addition property of equality and then the division property of equality.

Solve each equation. Round to the nearest hundredth if necessary.

36. $5 + \frac{2a}{-3} = \frac{5}{11}$
6.83

37. $\frac{3}{5}(p - 3) = -4$
−3.67

38. $11m - (6m - 5) = 25$
4

39. The sum of three integers is 228. The second integer is 1 more than the first, and the third integer is 2 more than the first. Write an equation to determine the integers. Solve your equation. Show your work.
$i + i + 1 + i + 2 = 228$; 75, 76, 77

40. Can you solve the equation $\frac{2}{3}(4x - 5) = 8$ by using the Division Property of Equality? Explain.
yes; divide both sides of the equation by $\frac{2}{3}$, which is the same as multiplying both sides of the equation by $\frac{3}{2}$.

Page 25

2-3 Practice Form K
Solving Multi-Step Equations

Solve each equation. Check your answer.

1. $20 + g + g = 14$ -3
2. $7 + 4x - 9 = -6$ -1
3. $-12 = -5 - 6n + 11$ 3
4. $t + 10 - 4t = -11$ 7
5. $8 = 8p + 13 - 3p$ -1
6. $4y - 16 + 8y = -4$ 1

Write an equation to model each situation. Then solve the equation.

7. A plumber finished three jobs on Tuesday. The first two only cost the owner the $45 trip fee because they took very little time to complete. For the third job, the plumber charged the trip fee plus 6 times his hourly rate. If the plumber received a total of $303 for the day, what is the hourly rate?
$45 + 45 + 45 + 6h = 303$; $28 per hour

8. Three times a number plus 12 minus 5 times the same number is 22. What is the number?
$3n + 12 - 5n = 22$; -5

Solve each equation. Check your answer.

9. $4(-2d - 3) = 12$ -3
10. $5(5t - 2) = -35$ -1
11. $-2(a + 6) = -22$ 5
12. $60 = 6(6 - 2n)$ -2
13. $-14 = -4(9x - 1)$ $\frac{1}{2}$
14. $-(5z + 12) = 18$ -6

Page 26

2-3 Practice (continued) Form K
Solving Multi-Step Equations

15. Eli took the fleet of 8 vans for oil changes. All of the vans needed windshield wipers which cost $24 per van. The total bill was $432. Write an equation to find out what each oil change cost. Solve the equation.
$8(v + 24) = 432$; $30

Solve each equation. Choose the method you prefer. Check your answer.

16. $\frac{m}{3} + \frac{1}{3} = \frac{2}{3}$ 1
17. $5r - \frac{1}{5} = \frac{4}{5}$ $\frac{1}{5}$
18. $\frac{w}{9} - 6 = \frac{7}{9}$ 61
19. $1.75t - 4.5 = 7.75$ 7
20. $6z + 0.36 = 24.72$ 4.06
21. $7.85 - 2.15c = 20.75$ -6

22. **Writing** Describe the first step you would take in solving $12 = 7 - 3x + 5x$. Explain.
First, you would combine the like terms $-3x$ and $5x$. This will result in having just one variable which needs to be isolated when solving.

23. **Writing** Describe how you would solve $-8 = \frac{1}{9}(-9t + 27)$.
The first way is to use the distributive property first by distributing the $\frac{1}{9}$ into $-9t + 27$ and then solving the resulting two-step equation. The second way is to use the multiplication property of equality and multiply each side by 9. The result is a two-step equation that can be solved.

Solve each equation. Round to the nearest hundredth if necessary.

24. $11 + \frac{4x}{-5} = \frac{2}{3}$ 12.92
25. $\frac{5}{7}(k + 5) = -7$ -14.8

26. **Reasoning** Can you solve the equation $\frac{3}{4}(6x + 9) = 14$ by using the Division Property of Equality? Explain.
Yes; for your first step, you would divide each side by $\frac{3}{4}$ or multiply by $\frac{4}{3}$. Then you can solve the two-step equation.

Page 27

2-3 Standardized Test Prep
Solving Multi-Step Equations

Multiple Choice

For Exercises 1–5, choose the correct letter.

1. What is the solution of $-17 = -2n + 13 - 8n$? C
   A. -3 B. $-\frac{2}{3}$ C. 3 D. 5

2. What is the solution of $-4(-3m - 2) = 32$? G
   F. -2 G. 2 H. 4 I. 6

3. What is the solution of $\frac{x}{3} + \frac{3}{5} = -\frac{1}{15}$? A
   A. -2 B. $\frac{8}{5}$ C. 2 D. $\frac{16}{3}$

4. When the sum of a number and 7 is multiplied by 4, the result is 16. What is the original number? G
   F. -12 G. -3 H. 3 I. 11

5. A merchant is selling wind chimes from a booth at a flea market. He rents his space for $125 per day. The profit from each wind chime sold is $12. His goal is to make $3500 in a five day work week. Which equation represents how many chimes he needs to sell in a week to meet his goal? A
   A. $12c - 625 = 3500$
   B. $5(12c) - 125 = 3500$
   C. $5(12c + 125) = 3500$
   D. $5(12c - 125) = 3500$

Short Response

6. Four friends are planning to play 18 holes of golf. Two of them need to rent clubs at $5 per set. Cart rental is $10. The total cost of the golf outing, including green fees, is $92. $2(5) + 10 + g = 92$; $72
   a. Write an equation to represent the total cost of the golf outing per player.
   b. How much did the friends pay in green fees?
   [2] Both parts answered correctly.
   [1] One part answered correctly.
   [0] Neither part answered correctly.

Page 28

2-3 Enrichment
Solving Multi-Step Equations

Consecutive integers are simply integers that follow each other in order. For example, 1, 2, and 3, are consecutive integers. Algebraically, these consecutive integers can be represented as follows:

$1 \rightarrow N$
$2 \rightarrow N + 1$
$3 \rightarrow N + 2$

Therefore, the sum of three consecutive integers is written as

$$N + (N + 1) + (N + 2)$$

So, consecutive even integers would be represented by $N, N + 2$, and $N + 4$, where N must be an even integer. Consecutive odd integers would also be represented by $N, N + 2$, and $N + 4$, where N must be an odd integer.

1. Find three consecutive even integers whose sum is 48.
   14, 16, and 18
2. Find three consecutive odd integers whose sum is 141.
   45, 47, and 49
3. Find three consecutive even integers whose sum is -240.
   $-82, -80, -78$
4. Find three consecutive odd integers whose sum is -465.
   $-157, -155$, and -153
5. Find three consecutive integers whose sum is 300.
   99, 100, and 101
6. Find three consecutive integers whose sum of the first and the third is -88.
   $-45, -44$, and -43
7. Find three consecutive integers for which 3 times the sum of the first and the third integers is -342.
   $-58, -57$, and -56
8. Find three consecutive even integers for which -4 times the sum of the first and the third integers is 192.
   $-26, -24$, and -22

Page 29

2-3 Reteaching
Solving Multi-Step Equations

To solve multi-step equations, use properties of equality, inverse operations, the Distributive Property, and properties of real numbers to isolate the variable. Like terms on either side of the equation should be combined first.

Problem

a) What is the solution of $-3y + 8 + 13y = -52$?

$-3y + 13y + 8 = -52$	Group the terms with y together so that the like terms are grouped together.
$10y + 8 = -52$	Add the coefficients to combine like terms.
$10y + 8 - 8 = -52 - 8$	To get the variable term by itself on the left side, subtract 8 from each side.
$10y = -60$	Simplify.
$\frac{10y}{10} = \frac{-60}{10}$	Divide each side by 10 since y is being multiplied by 10 on the left side. This isolates y.
$y = -6$	Simplify.

b) What is the solution of $-2(3n - 4) = -10$?

$-6n + 8 = -10$	Distribute the -2 into the parentheses by multiplying each term inside by -2.
$-6n + 8 - 8 = -10 - 8$	To get the variable term by itself on the left side, subtract 8 from each side.
$-6n = -18$	Simplify.
$\frac{-6n}{-6} = \frac{-18}{-6}$	Divide each side by -6 since n is being multiplied by -6 on the left side. This isolates n.
$n = 3$	Simplify.

Solve each equation. Check your answer.

1. $4 - 6h - 8h = 60$
   -4
2. $-32 = -7n - 12 + 3n$
   5
3. $14 + 12 = -15x + 2x$
   -2
4. $8(-3d + 2) = 88$
   -3
5. $-22 = -(x - 4)$
   26
6. $35 = -5(2k + 5)$
   -6
7. $3m + 6 - 2m = -22$
   -28
8. $4(3r + 2) - 3r = -10$
   -2
9. $-18 = 15 - 3(6t + 5)$
   1
10. $-5 + 2(10b - 2) = 31$
    2
11. $7 = 5x + 3(x - 2) + 5$
    1
12. $-18 = 3(-z + 6) + 2z$
    36
13. **Reasoning** Solve the equation $14 = 7(2x - 4)$ using two different methods. Show your work. Which method do you prefer? Explain.

    3; The first way of solving is better because there are fewer steps.

Page 30

2-3 Reteaching (continued)
Solving Multi-Step Equations

Equations with fractions can be solved by using a common denominator or by eliminating the fractions altogether.

Problem

What is the solution of $\frac{x}{4} - \frac{2}{3} = \frac{7}{12}$?

Method 1

Get a common denominator first.

$$\frac{3}{3}\left(\frac{x}{4}\right) - \frac{4}{4}\left(\frac{2}{3}\right) = \frac{7}{12}$$
$$\frac{3x}{12} - \frac{8}{12} = \frac{7}{12}$$
$$\frac{3x}{12} = \frac{15}{12}$$
$$\frac{3x}{12} \cdot \frac{12}{3} = \frac{15}{12} \cdot \frac{12}{3}$$
$$x = 5$$

Method 2

Multiply by the common denominator first.

$$12\left(\frac{x}{4} - \frac{2}{3}\right) = 12\left(\frac{7}{12}\right)$$
$$^3\cancel{12}\left(\frac{x}{\cancel{4}}\right) - ^4\cancel{12}\left(\frac{2}{\cancel{3}}\right) = \cancel{12}\left(\frac{7}{\cancel{12}}\right)$$
$$3x - 8 = 7$$
$$3x = 15$$
$$x = 5$$

Decimals can be cleared from the equation by multiplying by a power of ten with the same number of zeros as the number of digits to the right of the decimal. For instance, if the greatest number of digits after the decimal is 3, like 4.586, you multiply by 1000.

Problem

What is the solution of $2.8x - 4.25 = 5.55$?

$100(2.8x - 4.25 = 5.55)$	Multiply by 100 because the most number of digits after the decimal is two.
$280x - 425 = 555$	Simplify by moving the decimal point to the right 2 places in each term.
$280x = 980$	Add 425 to each side to get the term with the variable by itself on the left side.
$x = 3.5$	Divide each side by 280 to isolate the variable.

Solve each equation. Check your answer.

14. $\frac{x}{16} - \frac{1}{2} = \frac{3}{8}$ 14
15. $\frac{2a}{3} + \frac{8}{9} = 4$ $\frac{14}{3}$
16. $\frac{3n}{7} - 1 = \frac{1}{8}$ $\frac{21}{8}$
17. $-1.68j + 1.24 = 13$ -7
18. $4.6 = 3.5w - 6.6$ 3.2
19. $5.23y + 3.02 = -2.21$ -1

Page 31

2-4 ELL Support
Solving Equations with Variables on Both Sides

Choose the word from the list that best matches each sentence.

equation	identity	solution	variable

1. A placeholder for an unknown number. ___variable___
2. A value of the variable that makes the equation true. ___solution___
3. A mathematical sentence that states two quantities are equal. ___equation___
4. A mathematical sentence that is true for every value. ___identity___
5. In the equation $x + 12 = 34$, x is a ___variable___
6. A mathematical sentence that uses an equal sign, $=$, is called an ___equation___.
7. An ___equation___ that is true for every value is called an ___identity___.
8. $3x = x + 2x$ is an ___identity___ because it is true for all values of x.
9. A symbol, usually a letter, that represents one or more numbers is called a ___variable___.
10. In the equation $y - 15 = 34$, the number 49 is the ___solution___.

Circle all the variables in the equation.

11. $9\textcircled{w} - 7 = 3\textcircled{w} + 23$

12. $(5 - 6\textcircled{q}) = \frac{\textcircled{q}}{5} + 7$

Multiple Choice

13. Which of the following is an equation?
    - Ⓐ $3x - 6$
    - Ⓑ $5m$
    - Ⓒ $7w + 4 = 25$
    - Ⓓ $48 + 27y$

Page 32

2-4 Think About a Plan
Solving Equations With Variables on Both Sides

Skiing A skier is trying to decide whether or not to buy a season ski pass. A daily pass costs $67. A season ski pass costs $350. The skier would have to rent skis with either pass for $25 per day. How many days would the skier have to go skiing in order to make the season pass less expensive than daily passes?

Understanding the Problem

1. What do you know about the costs associated with buying a daily pass?

   the costs of a daily pass and a daily ski rental

2. What do you know about the costs associated with buying a season pass?

   the costs of a season pass and a daily ski rental

Planning the Solution

3. Write an expression using words to represent the cost of a daily pass. Write the algebraic expression.

   Let $d = $ the number of days you ski. $67d + 25d$

4. Write an expression using words to represent the cost of a season pass. Write the algebraic expression.

   Let $d = $ the number of days you ski. $350 + 25d$

5. How can you compare the cost of a daily pass with the cost of a season pass algebraically? What is the equation?

   write an equation to find when the costs are the same; $67d + 25d = 350 + 25d$

Getting an Answer

6. Solve the equation you wrote in Step 5. Show your work.

   $5\frac{15}{67}$

7. Explain what this solution means.

   The season pass is less if the person goes skiing 6 times or more.

Page 33

2-4 **Practice** Form G
Solving Equations With Variables on Both Sides

Solve each equation. Check your answer.

1. $3n + 2 = -2n - 8$
-2

2. $8b - 7 = 7b - 2$
5

3. $-12 + 5k = 15 - 4k$
3

4. $-q - 11 = 2q + 4$
-5

5. $4t + 9 = -8t - 13$
$-1\frac{5}{6}$

6. $22p + 11 = 4p - 7$
-1

7. $17 - 9y = -3 + 16y$
$\frac{4}{5}$

8. $15m + 22 = -7m + 18$
$-\frac{2}{11}$

9. $3x + 7 = 14 + 3x$
no solution

Write and solve an equation for each situation. Check your solution.

10. Shirley is going to have the exterior of her home painted. Tim's Painting charges $250 plus $14 per hour. Colorful Paints charges $22 per hour. How many hours would the job need to take for Tim's Painting to be the better deal? $250 + 14h = 22h$; more than $31\frac{1}{4}$ h

11. Tracey is looking at two different travel agencies to plan her vacation. ABC Travel offers a plane ticket for $295 and a rental car for $39 per day. M & N Travel offers a plane ticket for $350 and a rental car for $33 per day. What is the minimum number of days that Shirley's vacation should be for M & N Travel to have the better deal? $295 + 39d = 350 + 33d$; $d = 9\frac{1}{6}$; less than 10 days

Solve each equation. Check your answer.

12. $7(h + 3) = 6(h - 3)$
-39

13. $-(5a + 6) = 2(3a + 8)$
-2

14. $-2(2f - 4) = -4(-f + 2)$
2

15. $3w - 6 + 2w = -2 + w$
1

16. $-8x - (3x + 6) = 4 - x$
-1

17. $14 + 3n = 8n - 3(n - 4)$
1

Determine whether each equation is an *identity* or whether it has *no solution*.

18. $4(3m + 4) = 2(6m + 8)$
an identity

19. $5x + 2x - 3 = -3x + 10x$
no solution

20. $-(3z + 4) = 6z - 3(3z + 2)$
no solution

21. $-2(j - 3) = -2j + 6$
an identity

Page 34

2-4 **Practice** (continued) Form G
Solving Equations With Variables on Both Sides

Solve each equation. If the equation is an identity, write *identity*. If it has no solution, write *no solution*.

22. $6.8 - 4.2b = 5.6b - 3$
1

23. $\frac{1}{3} + \frac{2}{3}m = \frac{2}{3}m - \frac{2}{3}$
no solution

24. $-2(5.25 + 6.2x) = 4(-3.1x + 2.68)$
no solution

25. $\frac{1}{2}r + 6 = 3 - 2r$
$-\frac{6}{5}$

26. $0.5t + 0.25(t + 16) = 4 + 0.75t$
an identity

27. $2.5(2z + 5) = 5(z + 2.5)$
an identity

28. $-6(-p + 8) = -6p + 12$
5

29. $\frac{3}{8}f + \frac{1}{2} = 6(\frac{1}{16}f - 3)$
no solution

30. Three times the sum of a number and 4 is 8 less than one-half the number. Write and solve an equation to find the number.
-8

31. A square and a rectangle have the same perimeters. The length of a side of the square is $4x - 1$. The length of the rectangle is $2x + 1$ and the width is $x + 2$. Write and solve an equation to find x.
1

32. A movie club charges a one-time membership fee of $25 which allows members to purchase movies for $7 each. Another club does not charge a membership fee and sells movies for $12 each. How many movies must a member purchase for the cost of the two clubs to be equal?
$25 + 7n = 12n$; 5 movies

33. **Writing** Describe the difference between an equation that is defined as an identity and an equation that has no solution. Provide an example of each and explain why each example is an identity or has no solution.
Because $4x - 2 = 4x - 4 + 2$ is always true, the equation has infinitely many solutions and so it is an identity. Because $3y + 10 = 3y + 15$ is never true, the equation has no solution.

Page 35

2-4 **Practice** Form K
Solving Equations With Variables on Both Sides

Solve each equation. Check your answer.

1. $4y + 15 = 6y - 11$ 13

2. $5p + 6 = -4p - 8$ 14

3. $13k + 5 = k - 7$ -1

4. $6q - 1 = -q + 20$ 3

5. $25h + 40 = -15h - 80$ -3

6. $-2m + 13 = 2m - 3$ 4

Write and solve an equation for each situation. Check your solution.

7. Suzanne is going to rent a car while she is out of town. One car rental company offers a flat rate of $35 per day plus $0.10 per mile. Another car rental company offers the same car for $25 per day plus $0.25 per mile. She will need the car for 5 days. How many miles would she need to drive for the first rental company to be the better deal?
$5(35) + 0.1m = 5(25) + 0.25m$; more than 333.33 miles

8. Jeremy is looking at two different lawncare companies to weed and mulch his flower beds. Greenscape Lawncare offers to charge $100 for the mulch plus $12 per hr for the labor. D & J Landscape offers to charge $23 per hr for the job including the mulch. What is the minimum number of hours the job could be for D & J Landscape to have the better deal?
$100 + 12h = 23h$; 9 hours

Solve each equation. Check your answer.

9. $4(h + 2) = 3(h - 2)$ -14

10. $-(3b - 15) = 6(2b + 5)$ -1

11. $5x + 7 + 3x = -8 + 3x$ -3

12. $18 - 6a = 4a - 4(a + 3)$ 5

Page 36

2-4 **Practice** (continued) Form K
Solving Equations With Variables on Both Sides

Solve each equation. If the equation is an identity, write *identity*. If it has no solution, write *no solution*.

13. $6(4z + 2) = 3(8z + 4)$
identity

14. $-8t - 3t + 2 = -5t - 6t$
no solution

15. $-(8m + 4) = 4m - 2(6m + 2)$
identity

16. $-5(x + 7) = -5x + 35$
no solution

17. $5.5 - 3b = 2b - 6.25$
2.35

18. $\frac{3}{4} + \frac{1}{4}m = \frac{3}{4}m - \frac{1}{4}$
2

19. $-5(5.25 + 3.1x) = -6.2(2.5x + 1.9)$
no solution

20. $\frac{2}{3}h - 9 = 6 - \frac{2}{3}h$
$\frac{45}{4}$

21. $0.2f + 0.6(f + 20) = -8 + 0.4f$
-50

22. $-2(-w + 11) = -13 + 2w - 9$
identity

23. Six times the sum of a number and 3 is 12 less than 12 times the number. Write and solve an equation to find the number. $6(n + 3) = 12n - 12$; 5

24. A triangle with equal sides and a square have the same perimeters. The length of a side of the triangle is $2x + 2$. The length of a side of the square is $x + 8$. Write and solve an equation to find x. $3(2x + 2) = 4(x + 8)$; 13

25. **Open-Ended** Give one example of an equation with variables on both sides that is an identity and one equation with variables on both sides that has no solution. Justify your examples by solving the equations.
Answers may vary. Sample:
Identity: $-2x + 5 - 2 = 3 - 4x + 2x$
$-2x + 3 = -2x + 3$
$3 = 3$

No Solution: $5x + 6 - 3 = 7x - 2x + 4$
$5x + 3 = 5x + 4$
$3 \neq 4$

Page 37

2-4 Standardized Test Prep
Solving Equations With Variables on Both Sides

Multiple Choice

For Exercises 1–5, choose the correct letter.

1. What is the solution of $-8x - 5 + 3x = 7 + 4x - 9$? **B**
   A. -3 B. $-\frac{1}{3}$ C. $\frac{1}{3}$ D. 3

2. What is the solution of $-(-5 - 6x) = 4(5x + 3)$? **G**
   F. -2 G. $-\frac{1}{2}$ H. $\frac{1}{2}$ I. 2

3. What is the solution of $2n - 3(4n + 5) = -6(n - 3) - 1$? **A**
   A. -8 B. -6 C. $-\frac{1}{2}$ D. 4

4. Negative one times the sum of twice a number and 3 is equal to two times the difference of -4 times the number and 3. What is the number? **H**
   F. -4 G. -2 H. $-\frac{1}{2}$ I. 2

5. Jacob is saving for a new bicycle which costs $175. He has already saved $35. His goal is to have enough money saved in six weeks to pay for the bicycle. Which equation represents how much money he needs to save each week to meet his goal? **A**
   A. $35 + 6d = 175$
   B. $35 + 12d = 175$
   C. $6(35 + 2d) = 175$
   D. $2(35 + 6d) = 175$

Short Response

6. Admission for a water park is $17.50 per day. A season pass costs $125. A locker rental costs $3.50 per day.
   a. What is an equation that represents the relationship between the cost of a daily pass and the cost of a season pass? $17.50d \approx 125$
   b. How many days would you have to go to the water park for the season pass to save you money?
   Because $d = 7.1$, you would have to go to the water park at least 8 days.

   [2] Both parts answered correctly.
   [1] One part answered correctly.
   [0] Neither part answered correctly.

Page 38

2-4 Enrichment
Solving Equations With Variables on Both Sides

The circumference and area of a circle are determined by the formulas $C = 2\pi r$ and $A = \pi r^2$. An increase of 1 unit in the radius causes predictable increases in the circumference and area.

Start with a circle of radius 1 unit. Then $C = 2\pi$ units and $A = \pi$ square units. Increasing the radius by 1 unit, meaning $r = 2$, leads to $C = 4\pi$ units and $A = 4\pi$ square units. Increasing the radius by 1 unit again, meaning $r = 3$, leads to $C = 6\pi$ and $A = 9\pi$. You may notice a pattern emerging.

Even if the radius is not known, knowing by how much the radius changes makes it possible to compare the circumference and area of the new circle to the circumference and area of the old circle.

For a circle with radius x, $C = 2\pi x$ and $A = \pi x^2$.
If the radius is increased by 1 unit to $x + 1$, $C = 2\pi(x + 1)$ or $2\pi x + 2\pi$, and $A = \pi(x + 1)^2$ or $\pi(x^2 + 2x + 1)$.

1. The circumference of a circle is 8π cm. The radius is increased, and the circumference of the new circle is 16π cm. By how much was the radius of the original circle increased?
   radius increased by 4 cm

2. One circle has a radius 1 unit greater than another circle. The area of the larger circle is 9π square units greater than the area of the smaller circle. What are the radius and area of each circle?
   radii are 4 and 5; areas are 16π and 25π sq units

3. If the radius of a circle is increased by 1 unit, the area of the circle is increased by 16π square units. What is the radius of the original circle?
   7.5

4. By how many units must the radius of a circle be increased to increase its circumference by 22π units?
   11

5. The circumference of a circle is 4 times the circumference of a circle with a radius 1 unit less. What is the radius of each circle?
   radii are $\frac{4}{3}$ and $\frac{1}{3}$

Page 39

2-4 Reteaching
Solving Equations With Variables on Both Sides

To solve equations with variables on both sides, you can use the properties of equality and inverse operations to write a series of simpler equivalent equations.

Problem

What is the solution of $2m - 4 + 5m = 13 - 6m - 4$?

$7m - 4 = -6m + 9$ — Add the terms with variables together on the left side and the constants on the right side to combine like terms.

$7m - 4 + 6m = -6m + 9 + 6m$ — To move the variables to the left side, add $6m$ to each side.

$13m - 4 = 9$ — Simplify.

$13m - 4 + 4 = 9 + 4$ — To get the variable term alone on the left, add 4 to each side.

$13m = 13$ — Simplify.

$\frac{13m}{13} = \frac{13}{13}$ — Divide each side by 13 since x is being multiplied by 13 on the left side. This isolates x.

$m = 1$ — Simplify.

Problem

What is the solution of $3(5x - 2) = -3(x + 6)$?

$15x - 6 = -3x - 18$ — Distribute 3 on the left side and -3 on the right side into the parentheses by multiplying them by each term inside.

$15x - 6 + 6 = -3x - 18 + 6$ — To move all of the terms without a variable to the right side, add 6 to each side.

$15x = -3x - 12$ — Simplify.

$15x + 3x = -3x - 12 + 3x$ — To get the variable terms to the left side, add $3x$ to each side.

$18x = -12$ — Simplify.

$\frac{18x}{18} = \frac{-12}{18}$ — Divide each side by 18 since x is being multiplied by 18 on the left side. This isolates x.

$x = -\frac{2}{3}$ — Simplify and reduce the fraction.

Solve each equation. Check your answer.

1. $-5x + 9 = -3x + 1$
   4
2. $14 + 7n = 14n + 28$
   -2
3. $22(g - 1) = 2g + 8$
   1.5
4. $-d + 12 - 3d = 5d - 6$
   2
5. $4(m - 2) = -2(3m + 3)$
   $\frac{1}{5}$
6. $-(4y - 8) = 2(y + 4)$
   0
7. $5a - 2(4a + 5) = 7a$
   -1
8. $11w + 2(3w - 1) = 15w$
   1
9. $4(3 - 5p) = -5(3p + 3)$
   $\frac{27}{5}$

Page 40

2-4 Reteaching (continued)
Solving Equations With Variables on Both Sides

An equation that is true for every value of the variable for which the equation is defined is an identity. For example, $x - 5 = x - 5$ is an identity because the equation is true for any value of x. An equation has no solution if there is no value of the variable that makes the equation true. The equation $x + 6 = x + 3$ has no solution.

Problem

What is the solution of each equation?

a) $3(4x - 2) = -2(-6x + 3)$

$12x - 6 = 12x - 6$ — Distribute 3 on the left side and -2 on the right side into the parentheses by multiplying them by each term inside.

$12x - 6 - 12x = 12x - 6 - 12x$ — To get the variable terms to the left side, subtract $12x$ from each side.

$-6 = -6$ — Simplify.

Because $-6 = -6$ is always true, there are infinitely many solutions of the original equation. The equation is an identity.

b) $2n + 4(n - 2) = 8 + 6n$

$2n + 4n - 8 = 8 + 6n$ — Distribute 4 into the parentheses by multiplying it by each term inside.

$6n - 8 = 8 + 6n$ — Add the variable terms on the left side to combine like terms.

$6n - 8 - 6n = 8 + 6n - 6n$ — To get the variable terms to the left side, subtract $6n$ from each side.

$-8 = 8$ — Simplify.

Since $-8 \neq 8$, the equation has no solution.

Determine whether each equation is an *identity* or whether it has *no solution*.

10. $-3(2x + 1) = 2(-3x - 1)$
    no solution
11. $4(-3x + 4) = -2(6x - 8)$
    an identity
12. $3n + 3(-n + 3) = 3$
    no solution

Solve each equation. If the equation is an identity, write *identity*. If it has no solution, write *no solution*.

13. $-(4n + 2) = -2(2n - 1)$
    no solution
14. $2(-d + 4) = 2d + 8$
    0
15. $-k - 18 = -5 - k - 13$
    an identity

16. **Open-Ended** Write three equations with variables on both sides of the equal sign with one having no solution, one having exactly one solution, and one being an identity.
    Answers may vary. Sample: no solution: $3y + 7 = 3y - 12$; one solution: $3y + 7 = y - 12$; an identity: $2y - 10 + 5y = 7y - 10$;

ANSWERS

Page 41

2-5 ELL Support
Literal Equations and Formulas

There are two sets of cards below that show how to solve $12c + 2d = 48g$ for d.
The set on the left explains the thinking. The set on the right shows the steps.
Write the thinking and the steps in the correct order.

Think Cards

- Subtract 12c from each side.
- Divide each side by 2.
- Copy the problem.
- Simplify.
- Divide each term by 2 to simplify.

Write Cards

- $2d = 48g - 12c$
- $12c + 2d - 12c = 48g - 12c$
- $\frac{2d}{2} = \frac{48g - 12c}{2}$
- $d = 24g - 6c$
- $12c + 2d = 48g$

Think	Write
First, copy the problem.	**Step 1** $12c + 2d = 48g$
Second, subtract 12c from each side.	**Step 2** $12c + 2d - 12c = 48g - 12c$
Next, simplify.	**Step 3** $2d = 48g - 12c$
Then, divide each side by 2.	**Step 4** $\frac{2d}{2} = \frac{48g - 12c}{2}$
Finally, Divide each term by 2 to simplify.	**Step 5** $d = 24g - 6c$

Page 42

2-5 Think About a Plan
Literal Equations and Formulas

Density The density of an object is calculated using the formula $D = \frac{m}{V}$, where m is the object's mass and V is its volume. Gold has a density of 19.3 g/cm³. What is the volume of an amount of gold that has a mass of 96.5 g?

KNOW

1. What is the formula you are given for the density of an object?
$D = \frac{m}{V}$

2. What values are you given in the problem?
the density of gold is 19.3 $\frac{g}{cm^3}$; the mass of a certain amount of gold is 96.5 g.

NEED

3. What measurement are you asked to determine?
the volume of the gold

4. Solve $D = \frac{m}{V}$ for the variable V. Show your work.
$V = \frac{m}{D}$

PLAN

5. Write your new formula. Substitute the values you are given into the formula.
$V = \frac{96.5}{19.3}$

6. What is the volume of 96.5 g of gold?
5 cm³

7. In what units is your answer? Do these units make sense? Explain.
cm³; yes; $\frac{g}{\frac{g}{cm^3}} = cm^3$

Page 43

2-5 Practice Form G
Literal Equations and Formulas

Solve each equation for m. Then find the value of m for each value of n.

1. $m + 3n = 7; n = -2, 0, 1$
$m = 7 - 3n;$ 13; 7; 4;

2. $3m - 9n = 24; n = -1, 1, 3$
$m = 8 + 3n;$ 5; 11; 17;

3. $-5n = 4m + 8; n = -1, 0, 1$
$m = -\frac{5}{4}n - 2; -3\frac{1}{4}; -2; -\frac{3}{4};$

4. $2m = -6n - 5; n = 1, 2, 3$
$m = -3n - \frac{5}{2}; -5\frac{1}{2}; -8\frac{1}{2}; -11\frac{1}{2};$

5. $8n = -3m + 1; n = -2, 2, 4$
$m = -\frac{8n-1}{3}; 5\frac{2}{3}; -5; -10\frac{1}{3}$

6. $4n - 6m = -2; n = -2, 0, 2$
$m = \frac{1 + 2n}{3}; -1; \frac{1}{3}; 1\frac{2}{3}$

7. $-5n = 13 - 3m; n = -3, 0, 3$
$m = \frac{5n + 13}{3}; -\frac{2}{3}; 4\frac{1}{3}; 9\frac{1}{3}$

8. $10m + 6n = 12; n = -2, -1, 0$
$m = \frac{6 - 3n}{5}; 2\frac{2}{5}; 1\frac{4}{5}; 1\frac{1}{5};$

Solve each equation for x.

9. $fx - gx = h$
$\frac{h}{f - g}$

10. $qx + x = r$
$\frac{r}{q + 1}$

11. $m = \frac{x + n}{p}$
$pm - n$

12. $d = f + fx$
$\frac{d}{f} - 1$

13. $-3(x + n) = x$
$\frac{3}{4}n$

14. $\frac{x - 4}{y + 2} = 5$
$5y + 14$

Solve each problem. Round to the nearest tenth, if necessary. Use 3.14 for pi.

15. What is the width of a rectangle with length 14 cm and area 161 cm²?
11.5 cm

16. What is the radius of a circle with circumference 13 ft?
about 2.1 ft

17. A rectangle has perimeter 182 in. and length 52 in. What is the width?
39 in.

18. A triangle has base 7 m and area 17.5 m². What is the height?
5 m

Page 44

2-5 Practice (continued) Form G
Literal Equations and Formulas

Solve each problem. Round to the nearest tenth, if necessary.

19. To find the average number of points per game a player scores, use the formula Points Per Game = $\frac{Total\ Points}{Games}$. Find the number of games a player has played if she has scored a total of 221 points and is averaging 17 points per game. 13 games

20. Joan drives 333.5 miles before she has to buy gas. Her car gets 29 miles per gallon. How many gallons of gas did the car start out with? 11.5 gal

21. Stan is purchasing sub-flooring for a kitchen he is remodeling. The area of the floor is 180 ft² and the width of the kitchen is 12 ft. What is the length of the sub-floor? 15 ft

Solve each equation for the given variable.

22. $4k + mn = n - 3; n$
$\frac{-4k - 3}{m - 1}$

23. $\frac{c}{d} + 2 = \frac{f}{g}; c$
$d\left(\frac{f}{g} - 2\right)$

24. $3ab - 2bc = 12; c$
$-\frac{6}{b} + \frac{3a}{2}$

25. $z = \left(\frac{x + y}{3}\right)w; y$
$\frac{3z}{w} - x$

26. $-3(m - 2n) = 5m; m$
$\frac{3n}{4}$

27. $A = \frac{1}{2}bcd + bc; d$
$\frac{2(A - bc)}{bc}$

28. A room with width w, length l, and height h with four walls needs to be painted.
a. Write a formula for the area that needs to be painted not accounting for doors or windows. $A = 2lh + 2wh$
b. Rewrite the formula to find h in terms of A, l, and w. $\frac{A}{2l + 2w}$
c. If l is 18 ft, w is 14 ft and A is 512 ft², what is the height of the room? 8 ft
d. **Reasoning** Suppose l is equal to w. Write a formula for A in terms of w and h. $A = 4wh$

Page 45

2-5 Practice   Form K

Literal Equations and Formulas

Solve each equation for *y*. Then find the value of *y* for each value of *x*.

1. $y + 5x = 6; x = -1, 0, 1$
$y = -5x + 6;$ 11, 6, 1

2. $8x - 4y = -12; x = -3, -1, 1$
$y = 2x + 3;$ −3, 1, 5

3. $-3y = 2x - 9; x = -3, 0, 3$
$y = -\frac{2}{3}x + 3;$ 5, 3, 1

4. $5x = -y + 6; x = 1, 2, 3$
$y = -5x + 6;$ 1, −4, −9

5. $6y = -3x + 12; x = -4, -2, 0$
$y = -\frac{1}{2}x + 2;$ 4, 3, 2

6. $-5y + 10x = 5; x = -2, 0, 2$
$y = 2x - 1;$ −5, −1, 3

Solve each equation for *p*.

7. $xp + yp = z$ $\frac{z}{x+y}$

8. $n = \frac{p-k}{j}$ $nj + k$

9. $a = b + cp$ $\frac{a-b}{c}$

10. $\frac{p+3}{m} = -1$ $-m - 3$

Solve each problem. Round to the nearest tenth, if necessary. Use 3.14 for π.

11. What is the width of a rectangle with length 25 in. and area 375 in.²?   15 in.

12. What is the radius of a circle with circumference 5 cm?   0.80 cm

13. A triangle has base 15 ft and area 60 ft². What is the height?   8 ft

Page 46

2-5 Practice (continued)   Form K

Literal Equations and Formulas

Solve each problem. Round to the nearest tenth, if necessary.

14. In baseball, a player's batting average is calculated by using the formula
Average $= \frac{Hits}{At\ Bats}$. Find the number of times a player has batted if he has
24 hits and a batting average of approximately 0.320.   80 at bats

15. Dan drove 512 miles in 8 hours. What was his average speed for the trip?   64 mph

Solve each equation for the given variable.

16. $-2z - xy = x + 7$ for *x*
$x = \frac{2z + 7}{-y - 1}$

17. $\frac{a}{b} - 8 = \frac{c}{d}$ for *a*
$a = b\left(\frac{c}{d} + 8\right)$

18. $6qr + 7rs - 2st = -9$ for *r*
$r = \frac{-9 + 2st}{6q + 7s}$

19. $p = \left(\frac{m+n}{-5}\right)$ for *n*
$n = -5p - m$

20. A large box shaped like a rectangular prism needs to be painted.
  a. Write a formula for the area *A* to paint in terms of length *l*, width *w*, and
    height *h*. $A = 2lw + 2lh + 2wh$

  b. Rewrite the formula to find *l* in terms of *A*, *h*, and *w*. $l = \frac{A - 2wh}{2w + 2h}$

  c. If *h* is 36 in., *w* is 28 in. and *A* is 6112 in.², what is the length of the prism?   32 in.

Page 47

2-5 Standardized Test Prep

Literal Equations and Formulas

Multiple Choice

For Exercises 1–5, choose the correct letter.

1. What is the value of the expression $-2(3x - 2) + x + 9$ when $x = -3$?   C
  A. −16   **B.** −2   **C.** 28   **D.** 34

2. What is the value of the expression $6m + m - 4(-2m + 1 - m)$ when $m = -8$?   F
  F. −156   **G.** −92   **H.** −44   **I.** 36

3. What is the solution of $2d = \frac{a-b}{b-c}$ when you solve for *a*?   D
  A. $2d - b + c + b$
  B. $\frac{2d + b}{b - c}$
  C. $\frac{2d}{b - c} + b$
  D. $2d(b - c) + b$

4. A triangle has area 49.5 cm². If the base of the triangle is 9 cm, what is the
height of the triangle?   G
  F. 5.5 cm   **G.** 11 cm   **H.** 222.75 cm   **I.** 445.5 cm

5. A circle has circumference 10.99 yd. What is the radius of the circle? Round to
the nearest tenth if necessary. (Use 3.14 for π.)   A
  A. 1.8 yd   **B.** 3.5 yd   **C.** 7 yd   **D.** 34.5 yd

Short Response

6. The formula for the circumference of a circle is $C = 2\pi r$, where *r* is the radius
of the circle.
  a. What is the formula when solved for *r*? $r = \frac{C}{2\pi}$
  b. What is the radius of a circle with a circumference of 37.7 m? Round to the
    nearest tenth if necessary.   6 m

  [2] Both parts answered correctly.
  [1] One part answered correctly.
  [0] Neither part answered correctly.

Page 48

2-5 Enrichment

Literal Equations and Formulas

Celsius (used in other countries) and Fahrenheit (used is the U.S.) are the two
most commonly used scales for measuring temperature. Water freezes at 0°C and
at 32°F. The boiling point of water is 100°C and 212°F.

To convert temperature from Celsius to Fahrenheit, you can use the formula
$\frac{9}{5}C + 32 = F$, where *C* is degrees Celsius and *F* is degrees Fahrenheit.

1. Solve the above formula for *C* to find a formula you can use to convert degrees
Fahrenheit to Celsius. $C = \frac{5}{9}(F - 32)$

Use the formulas above for Exercises 2–6.

2. Convert 45°C to F.   **3.** Convert 45°F to C.
    113°F   7.2°C

4. Convert 20°F to C.   **5.** Convert 110°C to F.
    −6.7°C   230°F

6. Sherry lives in Baltimore and is pen pals with Lynn who lives in England. Lynn
tells Sherry that the average temperature for the past week in May was 25°C.
Sherry asked Lynn if she still needed her winter coat. What was Lynn's reply?
Explain.
  The temperature is 77°F, so Lynn didn't need her winter coat.

7. The formula for the volume of a pyramid is $V = \frac{Bh}{3}$ where *B* is the area of the
base and *h* is the height of the pyramid. Solve for *h*.
  $\frac{3V}{B} = h$

8. Use the formula you found in question 7 to determine the height of a pyramid
whose volume is 5 cm³ and the area of the base is 3 cm².
  5 cm

Page 49

2-5 Reteaching
Literal Equations and Formulas

A literal equation is an equation that involves two or more variables. When you work with literal equations, you can use the methods you have learned in this chapter to isolate any particular variable. To solve for specific values of a variable, simply substitute the values into your equation and simplify.

Problem

What is the solution of $4x - 5y = 3$ for y? What is the value of y when $x = 10$?

$4x - 5y - 4x = 3 - 4x$	To get the y-term by itself on the left side, subtract $4x$ from each side.
$-5y = -4x + 3$	Simplify.
$\frac{-5y}{-5} = \frac{-4x + 3}{-5}$	Divide each side by -5 since y is being multiplied by -5 on the left side. This isolates y.
$y = \frac{4}{5}x - \frac{3}{5}$	Simplify by dividing each term by -5. Notice, this changes the sign of each term.
$y = \frac{4}{5}(10) - \frac{3}{5}$	To find the value of y when $x = 10$, substitute 10 in for x.
$y = 7\frac{2}{5}$	Simplify by multiplying first, then subtracting.

When you rewrite literal equations, you may have to divide by a variable or variable expression. When you do so in this lesson, assume that the variable or variable expression is not equal to zero because division by zero is not defined.

Problem

Solve the equation $ab - bc = cd$ for b.

$b(a - c) = cd$	Since b is a factor of each term on the left side, it can be factored out using the Distributive Property.
$\frac{b(a - c)}{a - c} = \frac{cd}{a - c}$	To get b by itself, divide each side by $a - c$ since b is being multiplied by $a - c$. Remember $a - c \neq 0$.
$b = \frac{cd}{a - c}$	Simplify.

Solve each equation for y. Then find the value of y for each value of x.

1. $y + 5x = 2; -1, 0, 1$
   $y = 2 - 5x; 7; 2; -3;$
2. $6x = 2y - 4; 1, 2, 4$
   $y = 3x + 2; 5; 8; 14;$
3. $6x - 3y = -9; -2, 0, 2$
   $y = 2x + 3; -1; 3; 7;$
4. $4y = 5x - 8; -2, -1, 0$
   $y = \frac{5x - 8}{4}; -4\frac{1}{2}, -3\frac{1}{4}, -2;$
5. $3y + 2x = -5; 0, 2, 3$
   $y = \frac{-5 - 2x}{3}; -1\frac{2}{3}, -2\frac{1}{4}, -3\frac{2}{3};$
6. $5x = 8y - 6; -1, 0, 1$
   $y = \frac{5x + 6}{8}; \frac{1}{8}, \frac{3}{4}, 1\frac{3}{8}$
7. $3(y - 2) + x = 1; -1, 0, 1$
   $y = \frac{7 - x}{3}; 2\frac{2}{3}; 2\frac{1}{3}; 2;$
8. $\frac{x + 2}{y - 3} = 1; -1, 0, 1$
   $y = x + 5; 4; 5; 6;$
9. $\frac{y + 4}{x - 5} = -3; -2, 2, 4$
   $y = -3x + 11; 17; 5; -1;$

Page 50

2-5 Reteaching (continued)
Literal Equations and Formulas

A formula is an equation that states a relationship among quantities. Formulas are special types of literal equations. Some common formulas are shown below. Notice that some of the formulas use the same variables, but the definitions of the variables are different. For instance, r is the radius in the area and circumference of a circle and the rate in the distance formula.

Formula Name	Formula
Perimeter of a rectangle	$P = 2l + 2w$
Circumference of a circle	$C = 2\pi r$
Area of a rectangle	$A = lw$
Area of a triangle	$A = \frac{1}{2}bh$
Area of a circle	$A = \pi r^2$
Distance traveled	$d = rt$

Each of the formulas can be solved for any of the other unknowns in the equation to produce a new formula. For example, $r = \frac{C}{2\pi}$ is a formula for the radius of a circle in terms of its circumference.

Problem

What is the length of a rectangle with width 24 cm and area 624 cm²?

$A = lw$	Formula for the area of a rectangle.
$\frac{A}{w} = \frac{lw}{w}$	Since you are trying to get l by itself, divide each side by w.
$l = \frac{A}{w}$	Simplify.
$l = \frac{624}{24}$	Substitute 624 for A and 24 for w.
$l = 26$ cm	Simplify.

Solve each problem. Round to the nearest tenth, if necessary. Use 3.14 for π.

10. A triangle has base 6 cm and area 42 cm². What is the height of the triangle?
    14 cm
11. What is the radius of a circle with circumference 56 in.?
    about 8.9 in.
12. A rectangle has perimeter 80 m and length 27 m. What is the width?
    13 m
13. What is the length of a rectangle with area 402 ft² and width 12 ft?
    33.5 ft
14. What is the radius of a circle with circumference 27 in.?
    about 2.9 in.

Page 51

2-6 ELL Support
Ratios, Rates, and Conversions

Complete the vocabulary chart by filling in the missing information.

Word or Word Phrase	Definition	Picture or Example
ratio	A *ratio* compares two numbers by division, and can be written as $\frac{a}{b}$, a to b, or $a : b$, where b does not equal zero.	4 to 6, 4 : 6 , or $\frac{4}{6}$
rate	A *rate* is a *ratio* with two quantities with different units.	1. $\frac{\$10}{2 \text{ tickets}}$
unit rate	2. A *unit rate* is a ratio of two quantities with different units and for which the denominator is 1 unit.	$\frac{7 \text{ miles}}{1 \text{ hour}}$, $\frac{\$6.50}{1 \text{ ticket}}$
conversion factor	A *conversion factor* helps you change a value in one measurement unit to a value in a different measurement unit. A *conversion factor* is a ratio of two equivalent measures in different units.	3. $\frac{2.54 \text{ cm}}{1 \text{ in.}}$
numerator	4. The top number in a fraction is the *numerator*.	$\frac{24}{39}$ ←
denominator	The bottom number in a fraction is the *denominator*.	5. $\frac{1}{3}$ ←

Page 52

2-6 Think About a Plan
Ratios, Rates, and Conversions

Reasoning A traveler changed $300 to euros for a trip to Germany, but the trip was canceled. Three months later, the traveler changed the euros back to dollars. Would you expect that the traveler got exactly $300 back? Explain.

Know

1. What facts do you know about the situation?
   a traveler changed $300 to euros; 3 mo later, the traveler changed the euros
   back to dollars;

2. What circumstances would affect whether or not the traveler would receive exactly $300 back?
   whether or not there is a service charge; what the exchange rate is when
   the euros were converted back to dollars;

Need

3. What would you need to know to determine the amount of dollars the traveler would receive after three months?
   the exchange rate, the service charge

4. How do you convert the amount in euros to dollars?
   euros · $\frac{\text{dollars}}{\text{euros}}$

Plan

5. Once you have the information you need to answer the question, explain how you would determine the amount of dollars the traveler would receive in exchange for the euros.
   multiply the number of euros by the exchange rate and subtract any service
   charges

6. Would this process change over time? Explain.
   no; The values may change but not the process.

ANSWERS

Page 53

2-6 Practice — Form G
Ratios, Rates, and Conversions

Convert the given amount to the given unit.

1. 15 days; hours
360 h
2. 60 ft; yd
20 yd
3. 100 meters; cm
10,000 cm
4. 5 hr; min
300 min
5. 12 meters; ft
39.37 ft
6. 16 in.; cm
40.64 cm
7. 5 liters; qt
5.3 qt
8. 2076 cm; yd
22.7 yd
9. 15 pounds; grams
6803.85 g
10. 25 km; cm
2,500,000 cm
11. 3 mi; ft
15,840 ft
12. 60 min; s
360 s

13. The builder measures the perimeter of the foundation to be 425 ft. He must order steel beams to install around the perimeter of the foundation. Steel must be ordered in meters. How many meters of steel should the builder order?
129.6 m

14. Mrs. Jacobsen purchased a 5-pound package of ground beef for $12.40. She decided to use 8 ounces each day for dinner recipes. What was the cost of ground beef per meal?
$1.24 per meal

15. Car 1 drove 408 miles in 6 hours and Car 2 drove 365 miles in 5 hours during the cross-country road race. Who had the fastest average speed?
car 2

Copy and complete each statement.

16. 25 mi/hr = ___ m/min
570.6 m/min
17. 32 mi/gal = ___ km/L
13.6 km/L
18. 10 m/s = ___ ft/s
32.8 ft/s
19. 14 gal/s = ___ qt/min
3360 qt/min
20. 3.5 days = ___ min
5040 min
21. 100 yd = ___ m
91.4 m
22. 15 dollars/hr = ___ cents/min
25 cents/min
23. 5 L/s = ___ kL/min
0.3 kL/min
24. 62 in. = ___ m
about 1.6 m
25. 7 days = ___ s
604,800 s

Page 54

2-6 Practice (continued) — Form G
Ratios, Rates, and Conversions

26. Which weighs more, 500 pounds or 200 kilograms? 200 kg

27. Which is longer, 4000 ft or 1 kilometer? 4000 ft

28. Which is the better buy, 7 pounds for $8.47 or 9 pounds for $11.07? Explain.
$8.47 for 7 lb because it is the lower unit rate

29. A runner is running 10 miles per hour.
a. What conversion factors should be used to convert 10 mi/hr to ft/s?
$\frac{5280 \text{ ft}}{1 \text{ mile}}, \frac{1 \text{ hour}}{60 \text{ min}}, \frac{1 \text{ min}}{60 \text{ sec}}$
b. How many feet per second is the runner running?
about 14.7 ft/s

Determine if each rate is a unit rate. Explain.

30. $1.99 per pound
yes; the rate is $/lb
31. 100 feet per 2 seconds
no; the rate is not ft/s
32. 22 miles per gallon
yes; the rate is mi/gal

Find each unit rate.

33. 4 pounds of green peppers cost $7.56. $1.89/lb

34. Rahul travelled 348 miles in 6 hours. 58 mi/h

35. Cheryl assembled 128 chairs in 16 hours. 8 chairs/h

36. **Writing** Suppose you want to convert feet per second to miles per hour. What conversion factors would you use? How did you determine which unit should go in the numerator and which unit should go in the denominator of the conversion factors?
$\frac{60 \text{ s}}{1 \text{ h}}$ and $\frac{1 \text{ mi}}{5280 \text{ ft}}$; the answer is $\frac{\text{miles}}{1 \text{ hour}}$, so miles is the numerator and hours is the denominator

37. The volume of a box is 1344 cubic inches or in³.
a. How many cubic inches are in one cubic foot? Justify your answer.
1 cubic ft = 12 in. × 12 in. × 12 in. = 1728 in.³
b. What is the volume of the box in cubic feet? Justify your answer.
$1344 \text{ in.}^3 \cdot \frac{1 \text{ ft}^3}{1728 \text{ in.}^3} \approx 0.78 \text{ ft}^3$

Page 55

2-6 Practice — Form K
Ratios, Rates, and Conversions

Convert the given amount to the given unit.

1. 12 in.; cm 30.48
2. 528 cm; yd 5.77
3. 9 hr; min 540
4. 12 meters; cm 1200
5. 8 liters; qt 8.45
6. 7 days; hours 168
7. 10 pounds; grams 4535.92
8. 45 ft; yd 15
9. 10 meters; ft 32.81

10. A plumber needs to replace 20 feet of copper piping. When he gets to the supply store, the lengths are given in meters. How many meters of piping does he need to purchase? 6.1 m

11. An athletic director is laying out a rectangular soccer field to be 60 m wide and 95 m long. What are the dimensions of the field to the nearest whole yard?
66 yd wide by 104 yd long

Complete each statement.

12. 9 gal/s = 2160 qt/min
13. 5.5 days = 7920 min
14. 50 yd = 45.72 m
15. 10 mi/hr = 268.2 m/min
16. 25 mi/gal = 10.61 km/L
17. 5 m/s = 16.4 ft/s

Page 56

2-6 Practice (continued) — Form K
Ratios, Rates, and Conversions

18. Which weighs more, 5 ounces or 150 grams? 150 grams

19. Which is longer, 5 miles or 10 kilometers? 10 kilometers

20. Which is the better buy, 3 pounds for $8.31 or 5 pounds for $12.95? Explain.
5 pounds for $12.95 because the unit price is $2.59 and the unit price of the 3 lb is $2.77.

21. A cyclist is riding 18 miles per hour.
a. What conversion factors should be used to convert 18 mi/hr to ft/sec?
$\frac{1 \text{ hr}}{60 \text{ min}}, \frac{1 \text{ min}}{60 \text{ sec}}, \frac{5280 \text{ ft}}{1 \text{ mi}}$
b. How many feet per second is the cyclist riding? 26.4

Determine if each rate is a unit rate. Explain.

22. 3 liters per 60 seconds
no
23. 55 miles per hour
yes
24. $15 per hour
yes

Find each unit rate.

25. 5 pounds of apples cost $9.95. $1.99 per lb

26. The tub filled with 12 gallons of water in 5 minutes. 2.4 gal per min

27. Rocky earned $102 in 8 hours. $12.75 per hr

28. **Writing** Suppose you want to convert pounds to kilograms. What conversion factors would you choose to use? How did you determine which units should go in the numerators and the denominators of the conversion factors?
$\frac{5280 \text{ ft}}{1 \text{ mi}}, \frac{1 \text{ min}}{60 \text{ sec}}, \frac{1 \text{ hr}}{60 \text{ min}}$; The conversion factors must be set up with units in the numerator and denominator so that all of the units cancel each other leaving you with $\frac{\text{ft}}{\text{sec}}$.

Page 57

2-6 Standardized Test Prep
Ratios, Rates, and Conversions

Multiple Choice

For Exercises 1–6, choose the correct letter.

1. Which of the following rates is a unit rate? C
   A. $\frac{24\ in.}{1\ yd}$ B. $\frac{24\ in.}{2\ ft}$ C. $\frac{3\ ft}{1\ yd}$ D. $\frac{1\ ft}{12\ in.}$

2. How many centimeters are in 1 kilometer? I
   F. 0.000001   G. 0.00001   H. 10,000   I. 100,000

3. How many inches are in 3 yd 2 ft? C
   A. 60   B. 72   C. 132   D. 180

4. To convert miles per hour to feet per second, which conversion factor would not be used? I
   F. $\frac{1\ hr}{60\ min}$ G. $\frac{1\ min}{60\ sec}$ H. $\frac{5280\ ft}{1\ mi}$ I. $\frac{1\ mi}{5280\ ft}$

5. A healthy, adult cheetah can run 110 feet per second. How fast can a cheetah run in miles per hour? B
   A. 55   B. 75   C. 87   D. 161.3

6. Emmanuel was speaking with a friend from another country. His friend told him that the speed limit on most highways is 100 kilometers per hour in her country. This speed sounded fast to Emmanuel. Approximately what speed is this in miles per hour? F
   F. 62 mph   G. 65 mph   H. 70 mph   I. 100 mph

Short Response

7. Samantha earns $22 per hour as a plumbing apprentice. How much does she earn per minute in cents?
   a. What conversion factors would she use?
   $\frac{100\ cents}{1\ dollar} \cdot \frac{1\ h}{60\ min}$
   b. What amount does she earn per minute in cents?
   about 37 cents/min
   [2] Both parts answered correctly.
   [1] One part answered correctly.
   [0] Neither part answered correctly.

Page 58

2-6 Enrichment
Ratios, Rates, and Conversions

Nutritional information is placed on most food products. This data typically includes the number of calories, and the amount of protein, fat, or carbohydrates per serving. It may also include the amount of vitamins and minerals contained in the food.

Shown below are the nutrition information panels from a can of peanuts and a can of cashews. Both are dry roasted without salt.

Peanuts
Serving size . . . . 3 oz
Servings/container 4
Calories 510
Protein . . . . 21 g
Carbohydrates . . . . . . 18 g
Fat . . . . 42 g

Cashews
Serving Size . . . . 1.5 oz
Servings/container 8
Calories 240
Protein . . . . 6 g
Carbohydrates . . . . . . 13.5 g
Fat . . . . 19.5 g

1. Express the relationship of calories to ounces as a rate for the peanuts and cashews.
   peanuts: 170 calories/oz; cashews: 160 calories/oz

2. Express the relationship between grams of protein and ounces as a rate for the peanuts and cashews.
   peanuts: 7 g/oz; cashews: 4 g/oz

3. Express the relationship between grams of fat and ounces as a rate for the peanuts and cashews.
   peanuts: 14 g/oz; cashews: 13 g/oz

4. Based on your answer to Exercise 1, which product is lower in calories per ounce? How can you tell?
   cashews; the unit rate of calories/oz is less than peanuts

5. A friend wants to find products that are low in calories and fat and high in protein. Which would be the better choice for this friend—peanuts or cashews? Why?
   cashews; peanuts contain about twice as much fat

6. What factors must be considered when comparing nutrition information labels on different food products?
   the serving size, the unit rates

Page 59

2-6 Reteaching
Ratios, Rates, and Conversions

A unit rate is a rate with denominator 1. For example, $\frac{12\ in.}{1\ ft}$ is a unit rate. Unit rates can be used to compare quantities and convert units.

Problem

Which is greater, 74 inches or 6 feet?

It is helpful to convert to the same units. Conversion factors, a ratio of two equivalent measures in different units, are used to do conversions.

Multiply the original quantity by the conversion factor(s) so that units cancel out, leaving you with the desired units.

$6\ ft \times \frac{12\ in.}{1\ ft} = 72\ in.$

Since 72 in. is less than 74 in., 74 in. is greater than 6 ft.

Rates, which involve two different units, can also be converted. Since rates involve two different units, you must multiply by two conversion factors to change both of the units.

Problem

Jared's car gets 26 mi per gal. What is his fuel efficiency in kilometers per liter? You need to convert miles to kilometers and gallons to liters. This will involve multiplying by two conversion factors.

There are 1.6 km in 1 mi. The conversion factor is either $\frac{1.6\ km}{1\ mi}$ or $\frac{1\ mi}{1.6\ km}$.

Since miles is in the numerator of the original quantity, use $\frac{1.6\ km}{1\ mi}$ as the conversion factor so that miles will cancel.

$26\frac{mi}{gal} \times \frac{1.6\ km}{1\ mi}$

There are 3.8 L in 1 gal. The conversion factor is either $\frac{3.8\ L}{1\ gal}$ or $\frac{1\ gal}{3.8\ L}$.

Since gallons is in the denominator of the original quantity, use $\frac{1\ gal}{3.8\ L}$ as the conversion factor so that gallons will cancel.

$26\frac{mi}{gal} \times \frac{1.6\ km}{1\ mi} \times \frac{1\ gal}{3.8\ L} \approx 10.9\frac{km}{L}$

Jared's vehicle gets 10.9 kilometers per liter.

Page 60

2-6 Reteaching (continued)
Ratios, Rates, and Conversions

Exercises

Convert the given amount to the given unit.

1. 12 hours; minutes
   720 min
2. 1000 cm; km
   0.01 km
3. 45 ft; yd
   15 yd
4. 32 cups; gallons
   2 gal
5. 30 m; cm
   3000 cm
6. 15 lbs; kilograms
   6.81 kg
7. 42 in.; cm
   106.68 cm
8. 10 miles; km
   16.09 km
9. 25 ft; in.
   300 in.

10. Serra rode 15 mi in 1.5 hr. Phaelon rode 38 mi in 3.5 h. Justice rode 22 mi in 2.25 hr. Who had the fastest average speed?
    Phaelon

11. Mr. Hintz purchased 12 gallons of drinking water for his family for $14.28. He knows that this should last for 2 weeks. What is the average cost per day for drinking water for the family?
    $ 1.02/day

12. The unit price for a particular herb is 49 cents for 6 ounces. What is the price of the herb in dollars per pound?
    $ 1.31/lb

Copy and complete each statement.

13. 45 mi/h = ___ ft/s
    66 ft/s
14. 7 g/s = ___ kg/min
    0.42 kg/min
15. 50 cents/min = ___ $/h
    $ 30/h
16. 22 m/h = ___ cm/s
    0.6 cm/s
17. 15 km/min = ___ mi/h
    55.89 mi/h
18. 6 gal/min = ___ qt/h
    1440 qt/h

19. **Writing** Describe the conversion factor you would use to convert feet to miles. How do you determine which units to place in the numerator and the denominator?
    1 mile is the numerator and 5280 ft is the denominator; ft should cancel out so ft should be in the denominator

20. **Writing** Describe a unit rate. How do you determine the unit rate if the rate is not given as a unit rate. Illustrate using an example.
    A unit rate is a rate with a denominator of 1; divide both the numerator and denominator by the denominator; $\frac{5\ lbs}{\$3} = \frac{5 \div 3\ lb}{\$3 \div 3} = \frac{1.6\ lb}{\$1}$

Page 61

2-7 ELL Support
Solving Proportions

The column on the left shows the steps used to solve a proportion. Use the column on the left to answer each question in the column on the right.

Problem — Solving With a Proportion	
Twelve of the thirty-two students in the class voted to have the test on Thursday. What percent of the class voted for Thursday?	1. Read the title of the Problem. What does the title tell you? The problem will be solved with a proportion.
Write a proportion. $\frac{12}{32} = \frac{c}{100}$	2. What is a proportion? an equality between two ratios
Write the cross products. $12 \cdot 100 = 32 \cdot c$	3. What does writing the cross products mean? Multiplying the numerator of each fraction by the denominator of the other and setting the products equal to each other.
Simplify. $1200 = 32c$	4. What operation does $32c$ show? multiplication
Divide each side by 32. $\frac{1200}{32} = \frac{32c}{32}$	5. Why do you divide each side by 32? Division is the opposite of multiplication. Dividing by 32 undoes the multiplication by 32.
Simplify $1200 \div 32 = 37.5$. $37.5 = c$	6. Why can you write $\frac{1200}{32}$ as $1200 \div 32$? The fraction bar means divide.
Round to the nearest percent. $38 \approx c$	7. What does the symbol $\approx$ stand for? approximately equal to
Answer the question asked. Approximately 38% of the class voted for Thursday.	8. Why does the answer use the word approximately? The answer is not exact.

Page 62

2-7 Think About a Plan
Solving Proportions

Video Downloads A particular computer takes 15 min to download a 45-min TV show. How long will it take the computer to download a 2-hour movie?

Understanding the Problem

1. What facts do you know about the situation?
the time it takes to download a 45-min TV show

2. Are the units given in such a way that the numerators and the denominators of the proportion have the same units? If so, what are the units? If not, which units need to be converted?
no; convert h to min or min to h

Planning the Solution

3. If unit conversions are necessary, use conversion factors to convert the units. Show your work.
$2 \text{ h} \cdot \frac{60 \text{ min}}{1 \text{ h}} = 120 \text{ min}$

4. Write a proportion that can be used to determine the length of time necessary for the computer to download the movie.
$\frac{15 \text{ min}}{45 \text{ min}} = \frac{x \text{ min}}{120 \text{ min}}$

Getting an Answer

5. Solve the proportion you wrote in Step 4 to find how long it will take the computer to download the movie.
40 min

Page 63

2-7 Practice
Solving Proportions   Form G

Solve each proportion using the Multiplication Property of Equality.

1. $\frac{3}{5} = \frac{n}{6}$
9

2. $\frac{1}{5} = \frac{t}{3}$
$\frac{3}{5}$

3. $\frac{8}{3} = \frac{10}{9}$
$\frac{10}{3}$

4. $\frac{m}{4} = \frac{6}{5}$
$\frac{24}{5}$

5. $\frac{7}{6} = \frac{b}{2}$
$\frac{7}{3}$

6. $\frac{2}{9} = \frac{j}{18}$
4

7. $\frac{z}{3} = \frac{5}{4}$
$\frac{15}{4}$

8. $\frac{11}{12} = \frac{w}{15}$
$\frac{55}{12}$

9. $\frac{19}{10} = \frac{c}{23}$
43.7

Solve each proportion using the Cross Products Property.

10. $\frac{1}{4} = \frac{x}{10}$
$\frac{5}{2}$

11. $\frac{3}{n} = \frac{2}{3}$
$\frac{9}{2}$

12. $\frac{r}{12} = \frac{3}{4}$
9

13. $\frac{5}{y} = \frac{-3}{5}$
$\frac{25}{3}$

14. $\frac{-3}{4} = \frac{k}{16}$
-12

15. $\frac{22}{a} = \frac{-6}{5}$
$-\frac{55}{3}$

16. $\frac{15}{9} = \frac{8}{z}$
$\frac{24}{5}$

17. $\frac{11}{5} = \frac{q}{-6}$
$-\frac{66}{5}$

18. $\frac{f}{-18} = \frac{6}{-12}$
9

19. The windows on a building are proportional to the size of the building. The height of each window is 18 in., and the width is 11 in. If the height of the building is 108 ft, what is the width of the building? 66 ft

20. Eric is planning to bake approximately 305 cookies. If 3 pounds of cookie dough make 96 cookies, how many pounds of cookie dough should he make? 9.5 lb

21. On a map, the distance between Sheila's house and Shardae's house is 6.75 inches. According to the scale, 1.5 inches represents 5 miles. How far apart are the houses? 22.5 mi

Page 64

2-7 Practice (continued)
Solving Proportions   Form G

Solve each proportion using any method.

22. $\frac{n+4}{-6} = \frac{8}{2}$ -28

23. $\frac{10}{4} = \frac{z-8}{16}$ 48

24. $\frac{3}{t+7} = \frac{5}{-8}$ $-\frac{59}{5}$

25. $\frac{x-3}{3} = \frac{x+4}{4}$ 24

26. $\frac{3}{n+1} = \frac{4}{n+4}$ 8

27. $\frac{4d+1}{d+9} = \frac{-3}{-2}$ 5

28. Sixty-two students, out of 100 surveyed, chose pizza as their favorite lunch item. If the school has 1250 students, how many students would likely say that pizza is their favorite if the survey is a fair representation of the student body?
775 favor pizza

29. The senior class is taking a trip to an amusement park. They received a special deal where for every 3 tickets they purchased they received one free ticket. 3 tickets cost $53.25. The total purchase of tickets cost $1384.50. How many tickets did they receive?
104 tickets

Solve each proportion.

30. $\frac{x-1}{2} = \frac{x-2}{3}$
-1

31. $\frac{2n+1}{n+2} = \frac{5}{4}$
2

32. $\frac{3}{2b-1} = \frac{2}{b+2}$
8

33. **Open-Ended** Give one example of a proportion. Describe the means and the extremes of the proportion. Explain how you know it is a proportion. Give one non-example of a proportion. Explain how you know it is not a proportion.
Answers may vary. Sample:
$\frac{3 \text{ yd}}{2 \text{ dresses}} = \frac{12 \text{ yd}}{8 \text{ dresses}}$; The first and last terms, 3 yd and 8 dresses, are called the extremes; The middle terms, 2 dresses and 12 yd, are the means; non-example: $\frac{3}{2} = \frac{7}{6}$ is not a proportion because $3(6) \neq 2(7)$.

Page 65

2-7 Practice   Form K
Solving Proportions

Solve each proportion using the Multiplication Property of Equality.

1. $\frac{3}{4} = \frac{a}{12}$ 9

2. $\frac{1}{3} = \frac{m}{21}$ 7

3. $\frac{x}{5} = \frac{2}{3}$ 3.33

4. $\frac{f}{24} = \frac{3}{8}$ 9

5. $\frac{9}{7} = \frac{z}{126}$ 18

6. $\frac{3}{10} = \frac{b}{14}$ 4.2

Solve each proportion using the Cross Products Property.

7. $\frac{2}{5} = \frac{k}{18}$ 7.2

8. $\frac{4}{n} = \frac{6}{7}$ 4.67

9. $\frac{q}{-15} = \frac{1}{3}$ −5

10. $\frac{4}{d} = \frac{-1}{4}$ −16

11. $\frac{-13}{15} = \frac{k}{-5}$ 4.33

12. $\frac{-14}{h} = \frac{-2}{5}$ 35

13. On a scale drawing of a park, the length of a trail is 12 cm from the playground to the pond and 15 cm from the pond to the parking lot. If the actual length of the trail from the pond to the parking lot is 60 m, what is the actual length of the trail between the playground and the pond? 48 m

14. Jennifer is ordering cake for her wedding reception. If one cake will feed 18 people, how many cakes does she need to order for 150 people? 9 cakes

Page 66

2-7 Practice (continued)   Form K
Solving Proportions

15. Julie is drawing a map of the town. She knows that City Hall is 3 miles down Main St. from the fire station. If the scale for the map is 0.25 in.: 0.5 miles, how long should Main St. be between City Hall and the fire station on the map?
1.5 in.

Solve each proportion using any method.

16. $\frac{2}{j + 3} = \frac{4}{5}$ −$\frac{1}{2}$

17. $\frac{p + 1}{6} = \frac{6}{11}$ $\frac{25}{11}$

18. $\frac{-4}{5} = \frac{3}{z - 5}$ $\frac{5}{4}$

19. $\frac{15 - b}{6} = \frac{-2}{3}$ 19

20. A furniture factory makes 5 recliners for every 2 couches. If the factory makes a total of 154 recliners and couches in a day, how many recliners were made?
110 chairs

21. On the football team, two out of every seven players are seniors. If the team has 84 players, how many of the players are not seniors?
60 players

Solve each proportion.

22. $\frac{5}{n - 12} = \frac{-1}{n}$ $\frac{2}{3}$

23. $\frac{4v - 2}{8v} = \frac{2}{3}$ $\frac{3}{16}$

24. **Writing** Describe two different ways to solve $\frac{5}{6} = \frac{x}{24}$. Demonstrate both methods.
The two methods of solving the proportion are using the Multiplication Property of Equality and the Cross Products Property.

Multiplication Prop.:   Cross Products Prop.:

$24\left(\frac{5}{6}\right) = 24\left(\frac{x}{24}\right)$ $\frac{5}{6} = \frac{x}{24}$

$4(5) = x$ $6(x) = (5)(24)$

$20 = x$ $6x = 120$

$x = 20$

Page 67

2-7 Standardized Test Prep
Solving Proportions

Multiple Choice

For Exercises 1–5, choose the correct letter.

1. What is the solution to the proportion $\frac{3}{5} = \frac{x}{10}$? B

   A. $\frac{10}{3}$ B. 6   C. 10   D. 150

2. What is the solution to the proportion $\frac{x - 1}{x} = \frac{2}{3}$? H

   F. −2   G. 0   H. 2   I. 3

3. There are 105 members of the high school marching band. For every 3 boys there are 4 girls. Which proportion represents how many boys are in the marching band? A

   A. $\frac{3}{7} = \frac{b}{105}$ B. $\frac{3}{4} = \frac{b}{105}$ C. $\frac{4}{7} = \frac{b}{105}$ D. $\frac{7}{3} = \frac{b}{105}$

4. A baker is making bread dough. He uses 3 cups of flour for every 8 ounces of water. How many cups of flour will he use if he uses 96 ounces of water? I

   F. 4   G. 12   H. 32   I. 36

5. Mr. Carter offered to stay after school for an extra help session, and $\frac{2}{11}$ of his students stayed for the session. If there were 24 students that stayed for the help session, how many students does Mr. Carter teach throughout the day? C

   A. 100   B. 121   C. 132   D. 144

Extended Response

6. Elisabeth goes on a 5 mile run each Saturday. Her run typically takes her 45 minutes. She wants to increase this distance to 7 miles. Determine the proportion you use to find the time it would take her to run 7 miles. Solve the proportion. What proportion can be used to determine the time it takes for her to run a marathon, which is approximately 26 miles? What is her time?

   63 mi; 234 min

   [2] All parts answered correctly.
   [1] Some parts answered correctly.
   [0] No parts answered correctly.

Page 68

2-7 Enrichment
Solving Proportions

When dealing with right triangles, certain ratios are formed called trigonometric ratios. They are formed by examining various sides in relation to the angles. A commonly used triangle is the 30°-60°-90° triangle shown at the right. The hypotenuse is the side opposite the 90° angle. The other two sides are called sides opposite or adjacent to respective angles in the triangle.

Side a is opposite to angle A and adjacent to angle B. Side b is opposite to angle b and adjacent to angle A.

All 30°-60°-90° triangles are proportional, so the relationships shown in the triangle at the left can be used to determine missing lengths of any other 30°-60°-90° triangle provided you are given one side.

Use the relationships shown and proportions to determine the length of the other two sides.

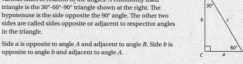

1. about 7.8 units; 4.5 units

2. 5.6 units; about 4.8 units

3.

4.

about 12.7 units; about 25.4 units   2x; 1.73x

Page 69

2-7 Reteaching
Solving Proportions

A proportion is an equation that states that two ratios are equal. If a quantity in a proportion is unknown, you can solve a proportion to find the unknown quantity as shown below.

Problem

What is the solution of $\frac{3}{4} = \frac{x}{14}$?

There are two methods for solving proportions—using the Multiplication Property of Equality and the Cross Products Property.

1) The multiplication Property of Equality says that you can multiply both sides of an equation by the same number without changing the value. $\frac{21}{4}$

$\frac{3}{4} = \frac{x}{14}$

$14\left(\frac{3}{4}\right) = \left(\frac{x}{14}\right)14$ To isolate x, multiply each side by 14.

$\frac{42}{4} = x$ Simplify.

$10.5 = x$ Divide 42 by 4.

2) The Cross Products Property says that you can multiply diagonally across the proportion and these products are equal. $\frac{10}{3}$

$\frac{3}{4} = \frac{x}{14}$

$(4)(x) = (3)(14)$ Multiply diagonally across the proportion.

$4x = 42$ Multiply.

$\frac{4x}{4} = \frac{42}{4}$ To isolate x, divide each side by 4.

$x = 10.5$ Simplify.

Real world situations can be modeled using proportions.

Problem

A bakery can make 6 dozen donuts every 21 minutes. How many donuts can the bakery make in 2 hours?

A proportion can be used to answer this question. It is key for you to set up the proportion with matching units in both numerators and both denominators.

For this problem, you know that 2 hours is 120 minutes and 6 dozen is 72 donuts.

Correct:
$\frac{72 \text{ donuts}}{21 \text{ min}} = \frac{x \text{ donuts}}{120 \text{ min}}$

Incorrect:
$\frac{72 \text{ donuts}}{21 \text{ min}} = \frac{120 \text{ min}}{x \text{ donuts}}$

Page 70

2-7 Reteaching (continued)
Solving Proportions

This proportion can be solved using the Multiplication Property of Equality or the Cross Products Property.

Problem

Solve this proportion using the cross products.

$\frac{72 \text{ donuts}}{21 \text{ min}} = \frac{x \text{ donuts}}{120 \text{ min}}$

$21x = (72)(120)$ Cross Products Property

$21x = 8640$ Multiply.

$\frac{21x}{21} = \frac{8640}{21}$ Divide each side by 21.

$x = 411.43$ Simplify.

Since you cannot make 0.43 donuts, the correct answer is 411 donuts.

Exercises

Solve each proportion using the Multiplication Property of Equality.

1. $\frac{3}{4} = \frac{n}{7}$ 2. $\frac{1}{3} = \frac{t}{10}$ 3. $\frac{n}{5} = \frac{8}{20}$
$\frac{21}{4}$ $\frac{10}{3}$ 2

4. $\frac{z}{6} = \frac{9}{8}$ 5. $\frac{15}{5} = \frac{a}{11}$ 6. $\frac{7}{2} = \frac{d}{8}$
$\frac{27}{4}$ 33   28

Solve each proportion using the Cross Products Property.

7. $\frac{3}{5} = \frac{b}{8}$ 8. $\frac{12}{m} = \frac{8}{3}$ 9. $\frac{z}{2} = \frac{9}{6}$
$\frac{24}{5}$ $\frac{9}{2}$ 3

10. $\frac{14}{b} = \frac{7}{3}$ 11. $\frac{-4}{-9} = \frac{f}{-12}$ 12. $\frac{13}{h} = \frac{2}{-6}$
6    $-\frac{16}{3}$ -39

13. A cookie recipe calls for a half cup of chocolate chips per 3 dozen cookies. How many cups of chocolate chips should be used for 10 dozen cookies?

$1\frac{2}{3}$

Solve each proportion using any method.

14. $\frac{x-3}{-2} = \frac{4}{5}$ 15. $\frac{12}{10} = \frac{y+6}{13}$ 16. $\frac{5}{x-3} = \frac{2}{-6}$
$\frac{7}{5}$ 9.6 -12

Page 71

2-8 ELL Support
Proportions and Similar Figures

Concept List

Cross Products Property	is congruent to	is similar to
length	proportion	ratio
scale	scale model	similar figures

Choose the concept from the list above that best represents the item in each box.

1. $24x = 10(18)$	2. $\sim$	3. $\frac{AB}{FG} = \frac{BC}{GH}$
Cross Products Property	is similar to	proportion
4. 1 cm : 12 m	5.	6. $\overline{RT}$
scale	similar figures	length
7. $\cong$	8. $\frac{16}{13}$	9.
is congruent to	ratio	scale model

Page 72

2-8 Think About a Plan
Proportions and Similar Figures

Trucks A model of a trailer is shaped like a rectangular prism and has a width of 2 in., a length of 9 in., and a height of 4 in. The scale of the model is 1 : 34. How many times the volume of the model of the trailer is the volume of the actual trailer?

Understanding the Problem

1. What is the formula you use to find the volume of a rectangular prism?
$V = lwh$

2. Using the scale, how can we find the dimensions of the actual trailer?
write a proportion with the scale as one side of the equation;

Planning the Solution

3. What is the volume of the model?
72 in.^{3}

4. Write three proportions that can be used to determine the actual length, height, and width of the trailer. Solve the proportions.
$\frac{1}{34} = \frac{2}{w}; \frac{1}{34} = \frac{9}{l}; \frac{1}{34} = \frac{4}{h}$

$25\frac{1}{2}$ ft; $5\frac{3}{3}$ ft; $11\frac{1}{3}$ ft

5. What is the volume of the actual trailer?
$1637\frac{2}{3}$ ft^3

Getting an Answer

6. How many times the volume of the model of the trailer is the volume of the actual trailer? Justify your answer.
volume of trailer is 39,304 times that of the model

Page 73

2-8 Practice   Form G
Proportions and Similar Figures

The figures in each pair are similar. Identify the corresponding sides and angles.

1. △ABC ~ △DEF

2. QRST ~ UVWX

AB and DE, BC and EF, AC and
DF, ∠A and ∠D, ∠B and ∠E,
∠C and ∠F

RS and VW, ST and WX, TQ and XU, QR
and UV, ∠R and ∠V, ∠S and ∠W, ∠T
and ∠X, ∠Q and ∠U

The figures in each pair are similar. Find the missing length.

3.

4.

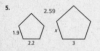

5.

6. 14.8   6.2   17.2   y   7.2

The scale of a map is 0.5 in. : 20 mi. Find the actual distance corresponding to
each map distance.

7. 2 in.   80 mi
8. 3.5 in.   140 mi
9. 4.75 in.   190 mi

10. A museum has a wax sculpture of a historical village. The scale is 1.5 : 8. If the
height of a hut in the sculpture is 5 feet, how tall was the original hut to the
nearest whole foot?   about 27 ft

11. On a map, the length of a river is 4.75 in. The actual length of the river is
247 miles. What is the scale of the map? $\frac{1 \text{ in.}}{52 \text{ mi}}$

Page 74

2-8 Practice (continued)   Form G
Proportions and Similar Figures

12. Sammy is constructing a model bridge out of sticks. The actual bridge is
1320 ft long. He wants the scale of his bridge to be 1 : 400. How long should the
model be?
  3.3 in.

13. The Finish-Line Company is drawing up plans for a room addition shown
below. The addition will include a large bedroom with a bathroom as shown.

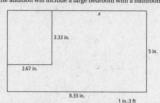

1 in.:3 ft

a. What are the actual dimensions of the room addition?
  24.99 ft by 15 ft
b. What are the actual dimensions of the bathroom?
  about 8 ft by 10 ft
c. What is the actual length of the exterior wall between the end of the room
addition and the bathroom wall? This length is represented by x.
  about 17 ft

14. Writing Are all right triangles similar? Explain your answer.
  Answers may vary. Sample: no; the right triangles formed by the
diagonal in a square are not similar to the triangles found by the
diagonal in a rectangle that is not a square.

15. Writing A pizza shop sells small 6 in. pizzas and medium 12 in. pizzas.
Should the medium pizzas cost twice as much as the small pizzas because
they are twice the size? Explain.
  The radius of the small pizza is 3 in., so its area is 9π. The radius of the larger
pizza is 6 in., so its area is 16π. They should charge four times as much.

Page 75

2-8 Practice   Form K
Proportions and Similar Figures

The figures in each pair are similar. Identify the corresponding sides and angles.

1. ABCD ~ EFGH

2. △MNO ~ △PQR

∠A and ∠E, ∠B and ∠F, ∠C and ∠G,
∠D and∠H; AB and EF, BC and FG, CD
and GH, AD and EH

∠M and ∠P, ∠N and ∠Q, ∠O
and ∠R; MN and PQ, NO and
QR, MO and PR

The figures in each pair are similar. Find the missing length.

3.

5.33

4.

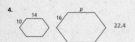

22.4

5.

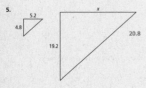

Page 76

2-8 Practice (continued)   Form K
Proportions and Similar Figures

The scale of a map is 0.25 cm : 15 km. Find the actual distance corresponding to
each map distance.

6. 0.75 cm   45 km
7. 2 cm   120 km
8. 3.5 cm   210 km
9. 5.25 cm   315 km

10. For a celebration a town is going to pass out miniature replicas of the town's
bell. The replicas are 9 in. tall. If the scale of the replica is 1 in. : 0.5 ft, how tall
is the actual bell?   4.5 ft

11. An architect created a scale model of what a college campus will look like
once construction is finished. The scale for the model is 2 in. : 25 ft. The tallest
building in the model is 10 in. tall. How tall is the actual building?   125 ft

12. A model of a golf course says that hole #9 is 175 yards long. If the scale of the
model is 2 in. : 20 yards, how many inches are there between the tee and the
hole on the model?   17.5 in.

13. Open-Ended Give an example of similar figures in your school.
  Answers may vary. See students' work.

14. Reasoning You are given two similar triangles. You know that one pair
of corresponding sides is equal. What do you know about the other sides?
Explain.
  The other sides are also equal. Since the corresponding angles
and one pair of corresponding sides is equal, the scale is 1 : 1.
The other pairs of corresponding sides are also equal.

Page 77

2-8 Standardized Test Prep
Proportions and Similar Figures

Multiple Choice

For Exercises 1–4, choose the correct letter.

1. The distance between Capeton and Jonesville is 80 miles. The scale on the map is 0.75 in. : 10 miles. How far apart are the cities on the map?   A
A. 6 in.   B. 60 in.   C. 600 in.   D. 1067 in.

2. The floor plan of a room has a scale of 2.5 in.: 35 ft. In the drawing, the length of the room is 8 in. and the width of the room is 6 in. What is the perimeter of the actual room?   I
F. 84 ft   G. 112 ft   H. 196 ft   I. 392 ft

3. The figures are similar. What is the missing length?   D
A. 9.33 cm
B. 5.4 cm
C. 6 cm
D. 21 cm

4. A model car is constructed with a scale of 1 : 15. If the actual car is 12 feet long, which proportion represents the length x of the model car?   A
F. $\frac{1}{15} = \frac{x}{12}$ G. $\frac{1}{15} = \frac{12}{x}$ H. $\frac{12}{15} = \frac{1}{x}$ I. $\frac{1}{12} = \frac{15}{x}$

Short Response

5. The scale of a map is 0.5 in. : 25 mi. The actual distance between two cities is 725 mi. Write a proportion that represents the relationship. How far apart will the cities be on the map?   14.5 in.

[2] Both parts answered correctly.
[1] One part answered correctly.
[0] Neither part answered correctly.

Page 78

2-8 Enrichment
Proportions and Similar Figures

You are an executive who has been given the privilege of designing your floor of the office building. Below is the outline of the floor plan for your floor. There are a few things shown that cannot be moved because they affect the other floors of the building.

The plan is drawn to a scale 1 in. : 18 ft and each unit on the grid represents 0.3 in.

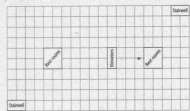

1. What are the actual dimensions of the entire office building?
144 ft by 336 ft

2. What is the actual size of the restrooms? elevators? stairwells?
24 ft by 24 ft; 12 ft by 24 ft; 12 ft by 24 ft;

3. You design the following on your floor: 2 break rooms, 2 copier rooms, 10 executive offices that are at least 18 ft by 12 ft, and enough cubicles (minimum size of 6 ft by 6 ft) for 50 employees. Draw each of the rooms to scale on the grid shown above. Label your drawings.
Check students' work.

4. What are the actual dimensions of each of the rooms you designed?
Check students' work.

5. The break room has ceramic tile covering the floor. How many square yards of tile is there in the break room?
Check students' work.

6. Describe two ways to compute the actual area of any room on the floor plan.
Use the scale to find the length and width. Then use the formula for area, $A = lw$. Each square has an area of 144 ft^2 so multiply the number of squares by 144.

Page 79

2-8 Reteaching
Proportions and Similar Figures

In similar figures, the measures of corresponding angles are equal, and the ratios of corresponding side lengths are equal. It is important to be able to identify the corresponding parts in similar figures.

Since $\angle A \cong \angle D$, $\angle B \cong \angle E$, and $\angle C \cong \angle F$, $\frac{AB}{DE} = \frac{BC}{EF}, \frac{AB}{DE} = \frac{AC}{DF}$. This fact can help you to find missing lengths.

Problem

What is the missing length in the similar figures?

First, determine which sides correspond. The side with length 14 corresponds to the side with length 16. The side with length x corresponds to the side with length 12. These can be set into a proportion.

$\frac{14}{16} = \frac{x}{12}$ Write a proportion using corresponding lengths.
$(16)(x) = (14)(12)$ Cross Products Property
$16x = 168$ Multiply.
$x = 10.5$ Divide each side by 16 and simplify.

Exercises

The figures in each pair are similar. Identify the corresponding sides and angles.

1.

AB and EF, BC and FG, CD and GH, HE and DA, $\angle A$ and $\angle E$, $\angle B$ and $\angle F$, $\angle C$ and $\angle G$, $\angle D$ and $\angle H$

2.
MN and PQ, NO and QR, OM and RP, $\angle M$ and $\angle P$, $\angle N$ and $\angle Q$, $\angle O$ and $\angle R$

Page 80

2-8 Reteaching (continued)
Proportions and Similar Figures

Exercises

The figures in each pair are similar. Find the missing length.

3.   4.

5.   6.

Problem

A map shows the distance between two towns is 3.5 inches where the scale on the map is 0.25 in. : 5 mi. What is the actual distance between the towns?

Map scale: $\frac{\text{map distance}}{\text{actual distance}}$

If you let x be the actual distance between the towns, you can set up and solve a the proportion to answer the question.

$\frac{0.25 \text{ in.}}{5 \text{ mi}} = \frac{3.5 \text{ in.}}{x \text{ mi}}$
$0.25x = 17.5$
$x = 70$

The towns are 70 miles apart.

Exercises

The scale of a map is 1.5 in. : 50 mi. Find the actual distance corresponding to each map distance.

7. 10 in.   8. 4.25 in.   9. 6.75 in.
333.3 mi $141\frac{2}{3}$ mi   225 mi

10. The blueprints of an octagonal shaped hot tub are drawn with a 1 in. : 5 ft scale. In the drawing the sides are 3.5 inches long. What is the perimeter of the hot tub?   140 ft

Page 81

2-9 ELL Support
Percents

Use the list below to complete the diagram.

$12 = p\% \cdot 36$	$\frac{a}{b} = \frac{p}{100}$	$I = 45(0.04)6$
$\frac{3}{4} = \frac{p}{100}$	$I = prt$	$a = p\% \cdot b$

The Percent Proportion

$\frac{3}{4} = \frac{p}{100}$

$\frac{a}{b} = \frac{p}{100}$

The Percent Equation

$a = p\% \cdot b$

$12 = p\% \cdot 36$

Simple Interest Formula

$I = prt$

$I = 45(0.04)6$

Page 82

2-9 Think About a Plan
Percents

Finance A savings account earns simple interest at a rate of 6% per year. Last year the account earned $10.86 in interest. What was the balance in the account at the beginning of last year?

Understanding the Problem

1. What is the formula for finding simple interest?
   $I = Prt$

2. What values are given in terms of the formula you wrote in Step 1?
   interest, rate, time

Planning the Solution

3. Substitute the given values into the formula for simple interest.
   $10.81 = P(0.06)(1)$

Getting an Answer

4. Solve for the unknown value.
   $ 181.00

5. Is your answer reasonable? Explain.
   yes; 6% of $ 200 is $ 12, so 6% of $ 181.00 would be about $ 12.

6. What does your solution mean?
   There was $ 181.00 in the account.

Page 83

2-9 Practice   Form G
Percents

Find each percent.

1. What percent of 42 is 28?
   $66\frac{2}{3}\%$

2. What percent of 48 is 18?
   37.5%

3. What percent of 150 is 350?
   $233\frac{1}{3}\%$

4. What percent of 99 is 72?
   73%

5. What percent of 15 is 12?
   80

6. What percent of 120 is 200?
   $166\frac{2}{3}\%$

Find each part.

7. What is 75% of 180?
   136

8. What is 40% of 720?
   288

9. What is 125% of 62?
   77.5

10. What is 50% of 821?
    410.5

11. What is 2.75% of 20?
    0.55

12. What is 16.5% of 33?
    5.445

13. A set of golf clubs that costs $600 are on sale for 40% off the regular price. What is the sale price of the clubs? $ 360

14. A discount store marks up the merchandise it sells by 55%. If the wholesale price of a particular item is $25, what should the retail price be set at? $ 38.75

15. A used car lot runs sales at the end of the year to reduce inventory. This year the sale price is 15% less than the regular price. If the regular price of a car is $12,000, what is the sale price of the car? $ 10,200

Page 84

2-9 Practice (continued)   Form G
Percents

Find each base.

16. 60% of what number is 75?
    125

17. 115% of what number is 120?
    about 104.3

18. 15% of what number is 6.75?
    45

19. 5% of what number is 4.1?
    82

20. 68% of what number is 64.6?
    95

21. 65% of what number is 577.2?
    888

22. If you deposit $800 in a savings account that earns simple interest at a rate of 1.5% per year, how much interest will you have earned after 5 years?   760

23. When Marty was born, his parents deposited $5000 in a college savings account that earns simple interest at a rate of 7.25% per year. How much interest will the money have earned after 18 years? $ 6525

24. You have $10,000 to deposit in a savings account that earns simple interest at a rate of 4.5% per year. How much interest will be in the account after 2 years? $ 900

Tell whether you are finding a *percent*, a *part*, or a *base*. Then solve.

25. What is 25% of 50?
    a part; 12.5

26. What percent of 18 is 63?
    a percent; 350%

27. What is 133% of 90?
    a part; 119.7

28. What is 44% of 88?
    a part; 38.72

29. What percent of 67 is 26.8?
    a percent; 40%

30. 42 is 14% of what number?
    the base; 300

Page 85

2-9 Practice
Percents
Form K

Find each percent.

1. What percent of 58 is 18? 31%

2. What percent of 36 is 27? 75%

3. What percent of 65 is 115? 177%

4. What percent of 45 is 42? 93.33%

Find each part.

5. What is 40% of 120? 48

6. What is 62% of 500? 310

7. What is 150% of 84? 126

8. What is 33% of 171? 56.43

9. A pair of pants that regularly costs $55 are on sale for 35% off the regular price. What is the sale price of the pants? $35.75

10. A friend purchases items from a wholesale website and resells them on her own website. She typically marks up her merchandise 40%. If she purchased an item for $15, what price should she set for the item? $21

Find each base.

11. 70% of what number is 63? 90

12. 55% of what number is 231? 420

13. 165% of what number is 132? 80

14. 8% of what number is 1.2? 15

Page 86

2-9 Practice (continued)
Percents
Form K

15. $13,000 is deposited into a savings account that earns simple interest at a rate of 6.5% per year. How much interest will the money have earned after 3 years? $2535

16. Erma has $175,000 in a retirement account that earns simple interest at a rate of 9% per year. How much interest will the money have earned after 25 years? $393,750

17. A family deposited $8000 into an account six years ago. The account earned simple interest at a yearly rate. So far the total interest earned is $1200. What is the rate for the account? 2.5%

Tell whether you are finding a *percent*, a *part*, or a *base*. Then solve.

18. 112 is 20% of what number?
base; 560

19. What is 126% of 50?
part; 63

20. What percent of 88 is 36.96?
percent; 42%

21. What percent of 22 is 33?
percent; 150%

22. What is 268% of 150?
part; 402

23. What is 50% of 1175?
part; 587.5

Page 87

2-9 Standardized Test Prep
Percents

Multiple Choice

For Exercises 1–5, choose the correct letter.

1. What percent of 92 is 23? C
   A. 0.25%   B. 4%   C. 25%   D. 400%

2. 60% of a number is 66. Which proportion best represents this relationship? F
   F. $\frac{66}{b} = \frac{60}{100}$ G. $\frac{a}{66} = \frac{60}{100}$ H. $\frac{60}{b} = \frac{66}{100}$ I. $\frac{60}{66} = \frac{b}{100}$

3. A store is having a clearance sale where merchandise on the sales racks is reduced by 80% from the original price. If a jacket was originally priced at $76, what is the sale price? A
   A. $15.20   B. $24.20   C. $60.80   D. $72.40

4. If you deposit $3000 in a savings account that earns simple interest at a rate of 2.5% per year, how much interest will you have earned after 4 years? G
   F. $30   G. $300   H. $3000   I. $30,000

5. Five years ago you deposited a sum of money into a savings account which has earned $150 in interest. The interest rate for the account is 3% simple interest per year. How much money was originally deposited in the account? C
   A. $22.50   B. $100   C. $1000   D. $10,000

Short Response

6. There are 3200 students at Martinsville High School. There are 575 students involved in athletics during the spring athletic seasons. What proportion represents the percent of students not involved in athletics during the spring season? What percent of students is not involved in athletics?

   $\frac{2625}{3200} = \frac{p}{100}$; about 82%

   [2] Both parts answered correctly.
   [1] One part answered correctly.
   [0] Neither part answered correctly.

Page 88

2-9 Enrichment
Percents

Compound Interest and Annual Percentage Yield

When money is invested in some types of accounts, such as savings accounts or certificates of deposit, the interest is compounded. This means that interest is paid at intervals, such as monthly, quarterly, or yearly. The interest is added to the account, and interest is then earned on the interest that has already been paid. For every $100 invested in an account paying 6% interest, compounded twice per year, the interest earned is $6.09. This represents a rate of 6.09%, because of the compounding.

The name for the effective percent earned on an account where the interest is compounded is annual percentage yield (APY). It tells what percent of an original investment you will earn in a year.

The equation that expresses this percent is APY $= \left(1 + \frac{i}{n}\right)^n - 1$, where i is the advertised interest rate (written as a decimal) and n is the number of compounding periods per year. The result is the percent, written as a decimal. Using the example above, with $i = 0.06$ and $n = 2$:

$$\text{APY} = \left(1 + \frac{0.06}{2}\right)^2 - 1$$
$$= 1.0609 - 1$$
$$= 0.0609$$
$$= 6.09\%$$

For Exercises 1–4, determine the annual percentage yield (APY).

1. 8% interest rate, 2 compounding periods per year 8.16%

2. 8% interest rate, 4 compounding periods per year 8.24%

3. 8% interest rate, 6 compounding periods per year 8.27%

4. 8% interest rate, 12 compounding periods per year 8.30%

5. What do you notice about the APY as the number of compounding periods increases? the APY increases

6. What is the relationship between the interest rate and the APY when the number of compounding periods per year is 1? What does this mean?
   they are the same; the interest is simple interest

Page 89

2-9 Reteaching
Percents

Percents compare whole quantities, represented by 100%, and parts of the whole.

Problem

What percent of 90 is 27?

There are two ways presented for finding percents.

1) You can use the percent proportion $\frac{a}{b} = \frac{p}{100}$. The percent is represented by $\frac{p}{100}$. The base, b, is the whole quantity and must be the denominator of the other fraction in the proportion. The part of the quantity is represented by a.

$\frac{27}{90} = \frac{p}{100}$ — Substitute given values into the percent proportion. Since you are looking for percent, p is the unknown.

$27(100) = (90)(p)$ — Cross Products Property

$2700 = 90p$ — Multiply.

$30 = p$ — Divide each side by 90 and simplify.

27 is 30% of 90.

2) The other way to find percents is to use the percent equation. The percent equation is $a = p\% \times b$, where p is the percent, a is the part, and b is the base.

$27 = p\% \times 90$ — Substitute 27 for a and 90 for b.

$0.3 = p\%$ — Divide each side by 90.

$30\% = p\%$ — Write the decimal as a percent.

27 is 30% of 90.

Exercises

Find each percent.

1. What percent of 125 is 50? 40%

2. What percent of 14 is 35? 250%

3. What percent of 24 is 18? 75%

4. What percent of 50 is 75? 150%

Problem

75% of 96 is what number?

In this problem you are given the percent p and the whole quantity (base) b.

$a = p\% \times b$ — Write the percent equation.

$a = 75\% \times 96 = 72$ — Substitute 75 for p and 96 for b. Multiply.

Page 90

2-9 Reteaching (continued)
Percents

Problem

28% of what number is 42?

You are given the percent p and the partial quantity a. You are looking for the base b.

$a = p\% \times b$ — Write the percent equation.

$42 = 28\% \times b$ — Substitute 28 for p and 42 for a.

$42 = 0.28 \times b$ — Write 28% as a decimal, 0.28.

$150 = b$ — Divide each side by 0.28.

Exercises

Find each part.

5. What is 32% of 250? 80

6. What is 78% of 130? 101.4

Find each base.

7. 45% of what number is 90? 200

8. 70% of what number is 35? 50

Problems involving simple interest can be solved using the formula $I = Prt$, where I is the interest, P is the principal, r is the annual interest rate written as a decimal, and t is the time in years.

Problem

You deposited $2200 in a savings account that earns a simple interest rate of 2.8% per year. You want to keep the money in the account for 3 years. How much interest will you earn?

$I = Prt$ — Simple Interest Formula

$I = (2200)(2.8\%)(3)$ — Substitute 2200 for P, 2.8% for r, and 3 for t.

$I = 184.8$ — Multiply.

You will earn $184.80 in interest.

Exercises

9. If you deposit $11,000 in a savings account that earns simple interest at a rate of 3.5% per year, how much interest will you have earned after 5 years? $1925

10. If you deposit $500 in a savings account that earns simple interest at a rate of 4.25% per year, how much interest will you have earned after 10 years? $212.50

Page 91

2-10 ELL Support
Change Expressed as a Percent

For Exercises 1–4, draw a line from each word in Column A to its definition in Column B. The first one is done for you.

Column A	Column B
percent	expresses an amount of change as a percent of an original amount
1. estimate	a ratio comparing a number to 100
2. markup	an approximate answer that is relatively close to an exact amount
3. ratio	a comparison of two numbers by division
4. percent change	the difference between the selling price and the original cost of an item: $50 − $42

For Exercises 5–7, draw a line from each word in Column A to its definition in Column B.

A store's cost for a sweater is $32. The store sells the sweater for $40. Then the store puts the sweater on sale for $36.

Column A	Column B
5. discount	The new amount minus the original cost. $40 − $32 = $8
6. amount of increase	The percent a quantity decreases from its original amount. $\frac{(\$40 − \$36)}{40} \times 100$
7. percent decrease	The difference between the original price and the sale price. $40 − $36 = $4

Page 92

2-10 Think About a Plan
Change Expressed as a Percent

Student Discounts You show your student identification at a local restaurant in order to receive a 5% discount. You spend $12 for your meal at the restaurant. How much would your meal cost without the discount?

Understanding the Problem

1. What information are you given in the problem? What are you looking to find?
   the percent discount, 5%, and the price after the discount, $12; looking to find the amount the meal would cost without the discount

2. Does this question represent an amount of increase or an amount of decrease? In general, how is the amount of increase or decrease determined?
   amount of decrease; divide the change by the original amount

Planning the Solution

3. What formula can you use to determine the solution?
   percent $= \frac{\text{decrease}}{\text{original price}}$

4. Substitute values from the problem into your formula using x for the unknown value.
   $0.5 = \frac{x}{(12 + x)}$

Getting an Answer

5. Solve for the unknown value.
   $0.63

6. Check your answer.
   $\frac{\$0.63}{12.63} = \frac{x}{100}$; $12.63x = 63$; $x =$ about 5%

7. Is your answer reasonable? Explain.
   yes; The answer is close to a 5% discount.

Page 93

2-10 Practice Form G
Change Expressed as a Percent

Tell whether each percent change is an increase or decrease. Then find the percent change. Round to the nearest percent.

1. Original amount: 10
New amount: 12
20%

2. Original amount: 72
New amount: 67
6.9%

3. Original amount: 36
New amount: 68
89%

4. Original amount: 23
New amount: 25
increase; 9%

5. Original amount: 83
New amount: 41
decrease; 51%

6. Original amount: 19
New amount: 30
increase; 58%

7. Original amount: 38
New amount: 45
increase; 18%

8. Original amount: 16
New amount: 11
decrease; 31%

9. Original amount: 177
New amount: 151
decrease; 15%

10. The price of the truck was advertised as $19,900. After talking with the salesperson, Jack agreed to pay $18,200 for the truck. What is the percent decrease to the nearest percent? 9%

11. The Ragnier's purchased a house for $357,000. They sold their home for $475,000. What was the percent increase to the nearest percent? 33%

12. The original price for a gallon of milk is $4.19. The sale price this week for a gallon of milk is $2.99. What is the percent decrease to the nearest percent? 29%

Find the percent error in each estimation. Round to the nearest percent.

13. You estimate that a building is 20 m tall. It is actually 23 m tall. 13%

14. You estimate the salesman is 45 years old. He is actually 38 years old. 18%

15. You estimate the volume of the storage room is 800 ft^3. The room's volume is actually 810 ft^3. 1%

Page 94

2-10 Practice (continued) Form G
Change Expressed as a Percent

A measurement is given. Find the minimum and maximum possible measurements.

16. A nurse measures a newborn baby to be 22 in. long to the nearest in.
21.5 in.; 22.5 in.

17. A bag of apples weighs 4 lbs to the nearest lb.
3.5 lb; 4.5 lb

18. Fencing sections come in lengths of 8 ft to the nearest foot.
7.5 ft; 8.5 ft

Find the percent change. Round to the nearest percent.

19. 16 m to $11\frac{1}{4}$ m 30%

20. 76 ft to $58\frac{1}{2}$ ft 23%

21. $215\frac{1}{2}$ lb to $133\frac{1}{4}$ lb 38%

22. $42.75 to $39.99 6%

23. $315.99 to $499.89 58%

24. $5762.76 to $4999.99 13%

The measured dimensions of a rectangle are given to the nearest whole unit. Find the minimum and maximum possible areas of each rectangle.

25. 4 cm by 7 cm
22.75 cm^2; 33.75 cm^2

26. 16 ft by 15 ft
224.75 ft^2; 255.75 ft^2

27. 5 m by 12 m
51.75 m^2; 68.75 m^2

The measured dimensions of a shape or a solid are given to the nearest whole unit. Find the greatest percent error of each shape or solid.

28. The perimeter of a rectangle with length 127 ft and width 211 ft. 0.3%

29. The area of a rectangle with length 14 in. and width 11 in. 8.3%

30. The volume of a rectangular prism with length 22 cm, width 36 cm, and height 19 cm. 6.4%

Page 95

2-10 Practice Form K
Change Expressed as a Percent

Tell whether each percent change is an increase or decrease. Then find the percent change. Round to the nearest percent.

1. Original amount: 25 decrease; 28%
New amount: 18

2. Original amount: 48 increase; 50%
New amount: 72

3. Original amount: 178 decrease; 24%
New amount: 136

4. Original amount: 17 decrease; 12%
New amount: 15

5. Original amount: 45 increase; 33%
New amount: 60

6. Original amount: 95 decrease; 5%
New amount: 90

7. A store sells a running suit for $35. Joey found the same suit online for $29. What is the percent decrease to the nearest percent? 17%

8. An online auction store started the bid on an item at $19. The item sold for $49. What was the percent increase to the nearest percent? 158%

9. The original price for a motorcycle was $11,000. The sale price this week is $9799. What is the percent decrease to the nearest percent? 11%

Find the percent error in each estimation. Round to the nearest percent.

10. You estimate that a tree is 45 ft tall. It is actually 58 ft tall. 22%

11. A carpenter estimates the wall is 20 ft tall. The wall is actually 18 ft tall. 11%

Page 96

2-10 Practice (continued) Form K
Change Expressed as a Percent

A measurement is given. Find the minimum and maximum possible measurements.

12. A patient weighs 178 lb to the nearest quarter pound. 177.75 lb; 178.25 lb

13. A board is cut to 28 in. to the nearest half in. 27.75 in.; 28.25 in.

Find the percent change. Round to the nearest percent.

14. $158.49 to $149.99 5%

15. $29\frac{1}{2}$ oz to $23\frac{1}{4}$ oz 21%

16. $12\frac{1}{4}$ hr to $13\frac{1}{2}$ hr 10%

17. 7 in. to $12\frac{1}{2}$ in. 79%

The measured dimensions of a rectangle are given to the nearest whole unit. Find the minimum and maximum possible areas of each rectangle.

18. 25 in. by 22 in.
526.75 in.^{2}; 573.75 in.^{2}

19. 5 m by 7 m
29.25 m^2; 41.25 m^2

The measured dimensions of a shape are given to the nearest whole unit. Find the greatest percent error of each shape.

20. The perimeter of a rectangle with length 15 cm and width 21 cm. 3%

21. The area of a triangle with base length 32 in. and height 25 in. 4%

Page 97

2-10 Standardized Test Prep
Change Expressed as a Percent

Multiple Choice

For Exercises 1–5, choose the correct letter.

1. Sam ran 3.5 miles on Saturday. On Wednesday, he ran 5.2 miles. What was his percent increase to the nearest percent? C
   A. 33%   B. 42%   C. 49%   D. 67%

2. A department store purchases sweaters wholesale for $16. The sweaters sell retail for $35. What is the percent increase to the nearest percent? I
   F. 19%   G. 46%   H. 54%   I. 119%

3. Josephine measured the room to be 125 ft wide and 225 ft long. What is the maximum possible area of the room? D
   A. 700 ft^2 B. 27,950.25 ft^2 C. 28,125 ft^2 D. 28,300.25 ft^2

4. You estimate the height of the flagpole to be 16 ft tall. The actual height of the flagpole is 18 ft. Which equation can be used to determine your percent error in the estimated height? G
   F. $\frac{16-18}{18}$ G. $\frac{|16-18|}{18}$ H. $\frac{|16-18|}{16}$ I. $\frac{16-18}{16}$

5. You estimate that a box can hold 1152 in^3. The box is actually 10.5 in. long, 10.5 in. wide, and 8 in. tall. What is the percent error in your estimation? Round to the nearest percent. B
   A. 23%   B. 31%   C. 42%   D. 77%

Short Response

6. You measure a tub shaped as a rectangular prism to be 3 ft wide, 4 ft long, and 2.5 feet tall to the nearest half foot. What are the minimum and maximum volumes of the tub? What is the greatest possible percent error in calculating the volume of the tub?
   7.5 ft^3; 47.25 ft^3; 57.5%

   [2] Both parts answered correctly.
   [1] One part answered correctly.
   [0] Neither part answered correctly.

Page 98

2-10 Enrichment
Change Expressed as a Percent

A newspaper advertisement describes an end of the season sale at a store. The ad says you can take an additional 40% off coats that are already marked down 60%.

1. Marco concluded that the ad was presenting a percent change of 100%. What is wrong with Marco's conclusion?
   If the change were 100%, the items would be free.

2. Demonstrate how you determine the percent change from the original cost to the final advertised sale price of a coat costing $100. What is the percent change? 76%

3. A bookstore is having a storewide sale where all books are 30% off the list price. There is a clearance shelf where the price is discounted an additional 50% off. What is the percent change of the final discount for books on the clearance shelf? 65%

4. A discount warehouse buys the products it sells and marks up the price by 75%. This weekend the product is being sold for 25% off the regular price. What is the percent change from the wholesale price for this product during the sale? 131%

5. This year there was a 35% increase in attendance for the holiday pageant over last year's attendance. Next year, the committee is planning for a 40% increase in attendance over this year's attendance. What is the percent change from last year's attendance to next year's attendance? 89%

6. The original price of a product is $70. The original price is discounted a certain percentage, but the discount sticker has fallen off. There is a storewide additional 30% off for all merchandise. The price rings up as $36.75 at the register. Write an equation that will determine the percent of the original discount. What is the original discount?
   $36.75 = 0.7(70 - 70d)$; 25% or $17.50

Page 99

2-10 Reteaching
Change Expressed as a Percent

A percent change occurs when the original amount changes and the change is expressed as a percent of the original amount. There are two possibilities for percent change: percent increase or perent decrease. The following formula can be used to find percents of increase/decrease.

$$\text{percent change} = \frac{\text{amount of increase or decrease}}{\text{original amount}}$$

Problem

In its first year, membership of the community involvement club was 32 members. The second and third years there were 28 members and 35 members respectively. Determine the percent change in membership each year.

From the first to the second year, the membership went down from 32 to 28 members, representing a percent decrease. The amount of decrease can be found by subtracting the new amount from the original amount.

$\text{percent change} = \frac{\text{original amount} - \text{new amount}}{\text{original amount}}$ Percent Change Formula for percent decrease.

$= \frac{32-28}{32}$ Substitute 32 for the original number and 28 for the new number.

$= \frac{4}{32} = 0.125$ Subtract. Then divide.

Membership decreased by 12.5% from the first year to the second year.

From the second to the third year, the membership increased from 28 to 35 members, representing a percent increase. The amount of increase can be found by subtracting the original amount from the new amount.

$\text{percent change} = \frac{\text{original amount} - \text{new amount}}{\text{original amount}}$ Percent Change Formula for percent increase.

$= \frac{35-28}{28}$ Substitute 28 for the original number and 35 for the new number.

$= \frac{7}{32} \approx 0.22$ Subtract. Then divide.

Membership increased by about 22% from the second year to the third year.

Exercises

Tell whether each percent change is an increase or decrease. Then find the percent change. Round to the nearest percent.

1. Original amount: 25
   New amount: 45
   increase; 80%

2. Original amount: 17
   New amount: 10
   decrease; 41%

3. Original amount: 22
   New amount: 21
   decrease; 5%

Page 100

2-10 Reteaching (continued)
Change Expressed as a Percent

Errors can occur when making measurements or estimations. Percents can be used to compare estimated or measured values to exact values. This is called relative error. Relative error can be determined with the following formula comparing the estimated value and the actual value.

$$\text{Percent error} = \frac{|\text{measured or estimated value} - \text{actual value}|}{\text{actual value}}$$

Problem

Mrs. Desoto estimated that her class would earn an average of $126 per person for the fundraiser. When the money was counted after the fundraiser ended, each student had raised an average of $138 per person. What is the percent error?

There are two values given in this situation. The estimated value is $126 per person. The actual value that each person raised was $138.

$\text{Percent error} = \frac{|\text{measured or estimated value} - \text{actual value}|}{\text{actual value}}$ Percent Error Formula

$= \frac{|126-138|}{138}$ Substitute 126 for the estimated value and 138 for the actual value.

$= \frac{|-12|}{138}$ Subtract.

$= \frac{12}{138}$ $|-12| = 12$

≈ 0.09 Divide.

There was a 9% error in her estimation.

Exercises

Find the percent error in each estimation. Round to the nearest percent.

4. You estimate that your baby sister weighs 22 lbs. She is actually 26 lbs. 15%

5. You estimate that the bridge is 60 ft long. The bridge is actually 53 ft long. 13%

6. You estimate the rope length to be 80 ft. The rope measures 72 ft long. 11%

7. A carpenter estimates the roof to be 375 ft^2. The rectangular roof measures 18 feet wide by 22 feet long. What is the percent error? 5%

Page 101

Chapter 2 Quiz 1
Form G

Lessons 2-1 through 2-5

Do You Know HOW?

Solve each equation. Check your answer.

1. $45 = 3b + 69$ -8

2. $\frac{1}{3}(c - 2) = \frac{7}{3}$ 9

Solve each equation. Justify your steps.

3. $7 - 5t = 17$ -2

4. $5 = \frac{1}{2}v - 3$
$5 = \frac{1}{2}v - 3$
$2 \times 5 = 2 \times \left(\frac{1}{2}v - 3\right)$ Mult. Prop. of Equal.
$10 = v - 6$ Simplify.
$10 + 6 = v - 6 + 6$ Add. Prop. of Equal.
$16 = v$ Simplify.

Solve each equation. If the equation is an identity, write *identity*. If it has no solution, write *no solution*.

5. $10\left(x + \frac{1}{2}\right) = 3x + 5 + 7x$ no solution

6. $\frac{n-1}{2} = 17$ 35

7. $2.8p = 11.2$ 4

Define a variable and write an equation to model each situation. Then solve.

8. The total cost for 8 bracelets, including shipping was $54. The shipping charge was $6. What was the cost of each bracelet? $6

9. One music download store charges a monthly fee of $10 plus $1 per song downloaded. Another music download store charges a monthly fee of $30 for all the songs you want to download.
   a. How many songs would you have to download from the first store for the cost to be the same as the second store? 20 songs;
   b. If you only download 15 songs per month, from which download store would you buy your music? at first store

Do You UNDERSTAND?

10. **Reasoning** When solving a multi-step equation, does it matter in which order the operations are performed? Explain.
   yes; you need to undo steps using the reverse order of operations

Page 102

Chapter 2 Quiz 2
Form G

Lessons 2-6 through 2-10

Do You Know HOW?

Convert the given amount to the given unit.

1. 6 min; seconds 360 s

2. 112 dollars; cents 112,000 cents

3. 3.5 lb ; ounces 56 oz

Solve each proportion. Explain your reasoning.

4. $\frac{x + 10}{4} = \frac{3}{2}$
   Cross products are equal so $2(x + 10) = 5(4)$. Distribute the 2, so $2x + 20 = 12$. Subtract 20 from each side, so $2x = -8$. Divide both sides by 2, so $x = -4$.

5. $\frac{5}{a} = \frac{10}{a + 1}$
   In a proportion, cross products are equal, so $a(10) = 5(a + 1)$. Using the distributive property, $10a = 5a + 5$. Subtract 5 from both sides, so $5a = 5$. Divide both sides by 5, so $a = 1$.

In the diagram, $\triangle ABC \sim \triangle PQR$. Find each side length.

6. BC 13.5

7. CA 15

8. What percent of 60 is 12? 20%

9. What is 30% of 70? 21

10. Your car gets 30 mpg on the highway. If gas costs $4.20 per gallon, how much does it cost to drive your car per mile? 14 cents

11. A gardener has a 15 ft^2 garden. If she increases to a 24 ft^2 garden, by what percentage does she increase the area of the garden? 60%

Do You UNDERSTAND?

12. How are ratios and proportions the same? How are they different?
   Ratios and proportions both compare numbers. Proportions are equations. Ratios are expressions. Ratios are used in proportions. A proportion sets two ratios equal.

13. **Error Analysis** The length of an object is exactly 20 cm. A student says that a measurement of 19 cm represents a percent error of 95%, while a measurement of 21 cm represents a percent error of 105%. Explain what the student did wrong. What are the correct percent errors?
   The first percent error is 5%. The second is 5%. The student divided the wrong measurement by the correct measurement. The student should divide the absolute value of the difference in the measurements by the correct measurements.

Page 103

Chapter 2 Chapter Test
Form G

Do You Know HOW?

Solve each proportion.

1. $\frac{2}{1.2} = \frac{5}{k}$ 3

2. $\frac{12}{48} = \frac{g}{20}$ 5

3. $\frac{m}{20} = \frac{5}{4}$ 25

Solve each equation. Check your answer.

4. $7y + 5 = 3y - 31$ -9

5. $\frac{1}{2}(t + 7) = 32$ 57

6. $\frac{2h - 6}{6} = \frac{2}{3}$ 5

7. A cheetah ran 300 feet in 2.92 seconds. What was the cheetah's average speed in miles per hour? 70 mi/h

The figures are similar. Find the missing length.

8.
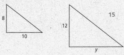

9. A tree casts a 26-ft shadow. A boy standing nearby casts a 12-ft shadow, forming similar triangles. His height is 4.5 ft. How tall is the tree? 9.75 ft

Tell whether each percent of change is an increase or decrease. Then find the percent of change.

10. Original amount: $90
   New amount: $84.50
   decrease; 6.1

11. Original amount: $100
   New amount: $140
   increase; 40%

12. Original amount: $15
   New amount: $5.50
   decrease; $63\frac{1}{3}$%

13. Original amount: $8.50
   New amount: $12.75
   50%

Page 104

Chapter 2 Chapter Test (continued)
Form G

Define a variable and write an equation to model each situation. Then solve.

14. An online music club sells compact discs for $13.95 each plus $1.95 shipping and handling per order. If Maria's total bill was $85.65, how many compact discs did Maria purchase?
   $13.95d + 1.95 = 95.65$; 6 discs

15. Tickets to the county fair for four adults and five children cost $33.00. An adult's ticket costs $1.50 more than a child's ticket. Find the cost of an adult's ticket.
   $4a + 5(a - 1.5) = 33$ or $4(c + 1.50) + 5c = 33$; $9.50

16. The scale of a map is 1 cm : 50 mi. Determine the distance between two cities that are 4.2 cm apart on the map.
   $\frac{10 \text{ m}}{50 \text{ mi}} = \frac{4.2 \text{ cm}}{a \text{ mi}}$; 210 mi

17. In 1995, the price of a laser printer was $1,299. In 2002, the price of the same type of printer had dropped to $499. Find the percent of decrease.
   $p = \frac{\text{change}}{\text{original amount}}$; 61.6%

Do You UNDERSTAND?

18. **Writing** Write a problem that can be solved using similar triangles. Draw a diagram and solve the problem.
   Check students' work.

19. **Open-Ended** Estimate your walking rate in feet per second. Write this rate in miles per hour.
   Check students' work.

20. **Reasoning** An item costs $64. The price is increased by 10%, then reduced by 10%. Is the final price equal to the original price? Explain.
   no; after the 10% increase, the item cost $64 + 0.10(64) = $64 + $6.40 = $70.40. After the discount, the item cost $70.40 - 0.10(70.40) = $70.40 - $7.04 = $63.36.

Page 105

Chapter 2 Part A Test
Lessons 2-1 through 2-5   *Form K*

Do You Know HOW?

Solve each equation. Check your answer.

1. $9g + 12 = 84$ 8   **2.** $\frac{1}{4}(z + 2) = \frac{3}{4}$ 1   **3.** $n + 11.2 = 25.1$ 13.9

4. $8x - 12 = 4x + 24$ 9   **5.** $\frac{1}{5}(x - 8) = x - 16$ 18   **6.** $\frac{x-4}{6} = \frac{5}{4}$ 11.5

Solve each equation. Justify your steps.

7. $8 + 6m = 26$

$8 + 6m - 8 = 26 - 8$	Subtraction Property of Equality
$6m = 18$	Simplify.
$\frac{6m}{6} = \frac{18}{6}$	Division Property of Equality
$m = 3$	Simplify.

8. $-6 = \frac{1}{5}y - 1$

$-6 + 1 = \frac{1}{5}y - 1 + 1$	Addition Property of Equality
$-5 = \frac{1}{5}y$	Simplify.
$5(-5) = 5\left(\frac{1}{5}y\right)$	Multiplication Property of Equality
$-25 = y$	Simplify.

Solve each equation. If the equation is an identity, write *identity*. If it has no real-number solution, write *no solution*.

9. $\frac{1}{3}(6x - 12) = 4\left(\frac{1}{2}x + 1\right) - 2$
no solution

10. $\frac{p-6}{2} = p - 4$

11. $2.6(t + 2) = 2(1.3t + 2) + 1.2$
identity

12. $2x + 4 = 5(x + 1) - 3(x + 2)$
no solution

13. Jackie earns $172 per week at her part time job. She is saving this money to buy a used car that costs $2000. At this rate, how many weeks will it take her to earn enough money to buy the car?   12 weeks

Solve each equation for the given variable.

14. $-3b + ac = c - 4$ for c
$c = \frac{-3b + 4}{1 - a}$

15. $\frac{x}{y} + 4 = \frac{z}{5}$ for x
$x = \frac{yz}{5} - 4y$

Page 106

Chapter 2 Part A Test (continued)
Lessons 2-1 through 2-5   *Form K*

Define a variable and write an equation for each situation. Then solve.

16. A large cheese pizza costs $7.50. Each additional topping for the pizza costs $1.35. If the total bill for the pizza Sally ordered was $12.90, how many toppings did she order? $1.35t + 7.5 = 12.90$; 3 toppings

17. A water park offers a season pass for $64 per person which includes free admission and free parking. Admission for the water park is $14.50 per person. Parking is normally $5 for those without a season pass.
  a. How many visits to the water park would you have to use for the season pass to be a better deal?   4 visits
  b. What would the total cost be for 3 visits with and without a season pass? $64 with a season pass; $58.50 without a season pass

18. The length of a rectangle is twice the width. An equation that models the perimeter of the rectangle is $2w + 4w = 36$ where w is the width of the rectangle in ft. What are the length and the width of the rectangle? $w = 6$ ft; $l = 12$ ft

19. Two consecutive odd integers can be modeled by n and $n + 2$, where n is an odd integer. The sum of two consecutive odd integers is 80. What are the integers?   39 and 41

Do You UNDERSTAND?

20. Writing Describe the steps that are involved in solving the equation $9 = 6 + \frac{z - 8}{4}$.
First, subtract 6 from each side. Multiply each side by 4. Add 8 to each side.

21. Open-Ended Write a multi-step equation for each condition listed below. Answers may vary. Check students' work.
  a. equation has no solution $3x + 4 = 6(x - 1) - 3(x + 2)$
  b. equation has one solution $3x + 4 = 6(x - 1) - 4(x + 2)$
  c. equation is an identity $3x - 12 = 6(x - 1) - 3(x + 2)$

Page 107

Chapter 2 Part B Test
Lessons 2-6 through 2-10   *Form K*

Do You Know HOW?

Convert the given amount to the given unit.

1. 8 ft; in.   96   **2.** 2.5 miles; ft   13,200   **3.** 260 sec; min $4\frac{1}{3}$

Solve each proportion. Use the Multiplication Property of Equality or the Cross Product Property. Explain your choice.

4. $\frac{1}{a} = \frac{6}{18}$ 3   **5.** $\frac{x+1}{15} = \frac{-4}{5}$ −13   **6.** $\frac{2}{q} = \frac{8}{q+12}$ 4

Solve each proportion.

7. $\frac{2.5}{10} = \frac{m}{4}$ 1   **8.** $\frac{14}{49} = \frac{4}{x}$ 14   **9.** $\frac{k}{10} = \frac{9}{6}$ 15

10. The figures at the right are similar. Find the missing length.   1.8 in.

11. What percent of 50 is 30?   60

12. What is 45% of 120?   54

Tell whether each percent change is an increase or decrease. Then find the percent change.

13. Original amount: $46   New amount: $52   increase; 13%

14. Original amount: $25   New amount: $35   increase; 40%

15. Original amount: $99.50   New amount: $92.50   decrease; 7%

16. Original amount: $19.25   New amount: $22.75   increase; 18%

Page 108

Chapter 2 Part B Test (continued)
Lessons 2-6 through 2-10   *Form K*

Define a variable and write an equation for each situation. Then solve.

17. There are 21 females in the Algebra 1 class. If 75% of the class is female, how many students are there in the class?   28

18. The scale of a map is 1 in. : 75 km. Determine the distance between two towns that are 5.6 in. apart on the map.   420 km

19. A flagpole casts a 32-ft shadow. A boy who is 6 feet tall is standing near the flagpole casting a 16-ft shadow. They form similar triangles. How tall is the flagpole?   12 ft

20. In 2005, a car sold new for $12,500. In 2008, value of the car was $8750. Find the percent decrease.   30%

Do You UNDERSTAND?

21. Error Analysis The average class grade went from 86% to an 81%. Susie thinks this represents a 5% change in the average. Explain Susie's error. What is the actual percent decrease?
5% represents the change in the grade, but the percent change is actually 5.8%.

22. Open-Ended Write a problem that can be solved using proportions. Write the proportion and solve the problem.
Check students' work

23. Writing Suppose you are given two similar triangles. All three side lengths of one triangle are given and one side length of the other triangle is given. Explain how you can find one of the missing side lengths. Include the steps for solving for the missing length.
Answers may vary. Sample: You can solve for the missing length by setting up a proportion by placing the lengths of the corresponding sides across from each other horizontally in the proportion. You solve the proportion by cross-multiplying diagonally and then dividing.

143

Page 109

Performance Tasks

Chapter 2

TASK 1

Suppose that you are the teacher. Look at the three equations below and provide a detailed description of how to solve each equation. Be sure to include in your discussion the different steps needed to solve each equation, and how the steps differ.

    a. $2x + 7 = 24$ **b.** $\frac{w}{4} - 2 = 12$ **c.** $\frac{5k + 3}{4} = -10$

    d. After you finish your discussion about the three equations above, you are anxious to show the class how these types of equations can model real-world situations. Write a description of two real-world situations: one that can be modeled by a one-step equation and one that can be modeled by a two-step equation. Write the equations and solve them. Check students work.

    [4] Student shows understanding of the task, completes all portions of the task appropriately with no errors in computation, and fully supports work with appropriate diagram and explanations.
    [3] Student shows understanding of the task, completes all portions of the task appropriately with one error in computation, and supports work with appropriate diagram and explanations.
    [2] Student shows understanding of the task, but makes errors in computation resulting in incorrect answer(s), or needs to explain better.
    [1] Student shows minimal understanding of the task or offers little explanation.
    [0] Student shows no understanding of the task and offers no explanation.

TASK 2

The relationship between the temperature in degrees Fahrenheit, F, and the temperature in degrees Celsius, C, is represented by the formula $F = \frac{9}{5}C + 32$.

    a. Solve the formula for C to express the Celsius temperature in terms of the Fahrenheit temperature. $\frac{5}{9}(F - 32) = C$

    b. A classmate tells you that there is one Fahrenheit temperature that is the same as the Celsius temperature. Is your classmate correct? If so, what is the temperature? If your classmate is incorrect, explain why. Yes; $-40°$

    [4] Sudent gives clear and correct calculations and explanations.
    [3] Student gives calculations and explanations that may contain same minor errors.
    [2] Student answers one part correctly and the other part has major errors.
    [1] Student gives calculations or explanations that contain major errors or omissions.
    [0] Student makes little or no efforts.

Page 110

Performance Tasks (continued)

Chapter 2

TASK 3

Solve one proportion using properties of equality. Solve the other using cross products. Explain the steps you used in each process.

    a. $\frac{x}{21} = \frac{4}{7}$ 12 $\frac{7}{4} = \frac{21}{x}$ 12

    b. Create a proportion that models a real-world situation. Be sure to define the variable, relate it to a model, write the equation, and solve the proportion. Check students' work.

    [4] Student shows understanding of the task, completes all portions of the task appropriately, and fully supports work with appropriate explanations.
    [3] Student shows understanding of the task, completes all portions of the task appropriately, and supports work with appropriate explanations with a minor error.
    [2] Student shows understanding of the task, but needs to explain better.
    [1] Student shows minimal understanding of the task or offers little explanation.
    [0] Student shows no understanding of the task and offers no explanation.

TASK 4

Michael has made a scale drawing of his classroom. The scale for his drawing is 0.5 in. : 3 ft.

    a. The length of the classroom is 30 ft. The length of the room on the scale drawing is 6 in. Is this correct? Explain why or why not. no; 5 in.

    b. One of the student tables is 6 ft long. How long should it be on the drawing? Explain how you got your answer. 1 in.; I solved the proportion $\frac{0.5\ in}{3\ ft} = \frac{x\ in}{30\ ft}$

    c. Write your own problem concerning Michael's drawing. Solve and explain your answers. Check students' work.

    [4] Student shows understanding of the task, completes all portions of the task appropriately with no errors in computation, and fully supports work with appropriate explanations.
    [3] Student shows understanding of the task, completes all portions of the task appropriately with one error in compuation, and supports work with appropriate explanations.
    [2] Student shows understanding of the task, but makes errors in computation resulting in incorrect answer(s), or needs to explain better.
    [1] Student shows minimal understanding of the task or offers little explanation.
    [0] Student shows no understanding of the task and offers no explanation.

Page 111

Cumulative Review

Chapters 1-2

Multiple Choice

For Exercises 1–10, choose the correct letter.

  1. Which algebraic expression represents 15 less than the product of 7 and a number? B
    A. $15 - 7n$ **C.** $15(7n)$
    B. $7n - 15$ **D.** $7(n - 15)$

  2. Which of the following is the correct simplification of $7 \cdot 4^2 \div 8 - 12$? I
    F. -28 **G.** $-\frac{17}{2}$ **H.** -5 **I.** 2

  3. What is the value of $\frac{3m^2 - mn}{2mn^2}$ when $m = -1$ and $n = 2$? A
    A. $-\frac{5}{8}$ **B.** $-\frac{1}{8}$ **C.** $\frac{1}{8}$ **D.** $\frac{5}{8}$

  4. What is the solution of $-6x + 15 = -3$? H
    F. -3 **G.** -2 **H.** 3 **I.** 6

  5. What is the solution of $4x - 6 = -6x - 4$? C
    A. $-\frac{3}{2}$ **B.** -1 **C.** $\frac{1}{5}$ **D.** 1

  6. What is the solution of $\frac{3}{5} = \frac{x}{15}$? H
    F. 1 **G.** 6 **H.** 9 **I.** 25

  7. A scale drawing of a building has the scale 0.5 in. : 6 ft. A wall is 30 ft long. How long will the wall be on the drawing? B
    A. 1.5 in.   **B.** 2.5 in.   **C.** 6 in.   **D.** 360 in.

  8. What is the simplified form of the expression $\sqrt{225}$? G
    F. -25 **G.** 15   **H.** 20   **I.** does not simplify

  9. Which property is illustrated by $45 + 19 = 19 + 45$? A
    A. Commutative Property of Addition   **C.** Associative Property of Addition
    B. Identity Property of Addition   **D.** Zero Property of Addition

  10. What percent of 86 is 50 to the nearest whole percent? G
    F. 43%   **G.** 58%   **H.** 59%   **I.** 172%

Page 112

Cumulative Review (continued)

Chapters 1-2

  11. A store's cost for a stereo was $27. The markup was 75%. A customer purchased it on sale at 40% off the marked up price. What was the purchase price of the stereo? $28.35

  12. Evaluate each expression for $x = 3$ and $y = 2$.
    a. $-4x + 3y$ -6 **b.** $\frac{x^2 - y}{4x}$ $\frac{7}{12}$

  13. Find the percent of decrease for each situation.
    a. $250 is discounted to $212.50 15%   **b.** $40 is discounted to $32 20%

  14. The school choir has 84 members. The ratio of girls to boys in the choir is 3 : 4. How many members are girls? 36 girls

Find each answer.

  15. Solve: $-2(3x + 2) = 2x + 6$ $-\frac{5}{4}$ **16.** Simplify: $-\sqrt{169}$ -13

  17. Solve: $\frac{3}{4} = \frac{8}{x - 1}$ $\frac{35}{3}$ **18.** Simplify: $14 + 2 \times 8 - 5^2 + 3^2$ 14

  19. Solve: $6n - 7 = 35$ 7   **20.** Solve: $\frac{x - 1}{2} = \frac{x + 3}{-1}$ $-\frac{5}{3}$

  21. The scale of a map is 0.25 cm : 15 mi. Determine the distance between two cities that are 6.8 cm apart on the map. 408 mi

  22. The price of the car was marked as $14,000. The end of the month sale has lowered the price to $12,500. What is the percent decrease to the nearest percent? about 10.7%

  23. Four times the sum of a number and -3 is 4 more than twice the number. Write and solve an equation to find the number. $4(n + (-3)) = 2n + 4$; 8

  24. Jeremy is putting together a model rocket. The scale is 1 cm : 50 ft. If the height of the actual rocket is 210 feet, how tall is the model? 4.2 cm

  25. Writing Describe four different subsets of real numbers. Explain the differences between the various subsets. Give several examples of each subset. The counting numbers are 1, 2, 3, 4, etc. The whole numbers are the counting numbers plus zero. Integers are the whole numbers and their opposites. Fractions are numbers used to express parts of the integers.

Page 113

Chapter 2 Project Teacher Notes: The Big Dig!

About the Project

The project gives students an opportunity to explore the mathematical connection between height and lengths of bones in the human body. The activities will help students understand how to measure and display data.

Introducing the Project

- Ask students to work with partners or in small groups. Students will need to know that the tibia is the inner and thicker of the two bones between the knee and the ankle, the humerus extends from the shoulder to the elbow, and the radius connects the wrist to the elbow.
- Discuss what tools and/or methods are available for measuring. Determine which would be best for this project and why. Discuss and evaluate ways to organize and display the data. Suggest that students create spreadsheets for calculating and displaying their information.

Activity 1: Graphing

Students list the lengths of the radius bones of all students and graph the data.

Activity 2: Calculating

Students calculate their own heights using the given formulas. Then they make suppositions about an archaeological find.

Activity 3: Analyzing

Students organize the data from Activity 1 by gender, then display the data to compare heights of males and females.

Activity 4: Creating

Students measure the tibia, humerus, and radius bones, and the heights of several adults. They organize their data on spreadsheets. Using the formulas from Activity 2, they predict heights and compare predictions with measured heights.

Finishing the Project

You may wish to plan a project day on which students share their completed projects. Encourage groups to explain their processes as well as their results. Have students review their project work and update their folders.

- Have students review their methods for finding, recording, and displaying the data they needed for the project.
- Ask groups to share insights that resulted from completing the project, such as any shortcuts they found for creating graphs and spreadsheets. Also, ask if any mathematical ideas have become more obvious, and whether there are areas about which they would like to learn more.

Page 114

Chapter 2 Project: The Big Dig!

Beginning the Chapter Project

Your bones tell a lot about your body. Archaeologists and forensic scientists study bones to estimate a person's height, build, and age. These data are helpful in learning about ancient people and in solving crimes. The lengths of major bones, such as the humerus, radius, and tibia, can be substituted into formulas to estimate a person's height.

As you work through the activities, you will collect data from your classmates and from adults. You will use formulas to analyze the data and predict heights. Then you will decide how to organize and display your results in graphs and spreadsheets.

List of Materials

- Calculator
- Tape measure or ruler
- Graph paper

Activities

Activity 1: Graphing

In this activity, you will collect, graph, and analyze data.

- Measure the length of your radius bone to the nearest half inch.
- Collect the measurements taken by your classmates. (Note whether each measurement is that of a male or a female for Activity 3.) Display the data in a graph.
- Write a description of the data.

Activity 2: Calculating

Scientists use the formulas in the table at the right to approximate a person's height H, in inches, when they know the length of the tibia t, the humerus h, or the radius r.

- Use your tibia, humerus, and radius bone lengths to calculate your height. Are the calculated heights close to your actual height? Explain.
- An archaeologist found an 18-inch tibia on the site of an American colonial farm. Do you think it belonged to a man or woman? Why?
- Choose one radius measurement from the data you collected for Activity 1. Calculate the person's height. Can you tell whose height you have found? Explain.

Male	
$H = 32.2 + 2.4t$	
$H = 29.0 + 3.0h$	
$H = 31.7 + 3.7r$	
Female	
$H = 28.6 + 2.5t$	
$H = 25.6 + 3.1h$	
$H = 28.9 + 3.9r$	

Page 115

Chapter 2 Project: The Big Dig! (continued)

Activity 3: Analyzing

When predicting height, scientists use different formulas for men and women.

- Review the data collected in Activity 1. Organize the data by male and female.
- Organize and display the data to see if there are differences between the heights of males and females.

Activity 4: Creating

In this activity, you will analyze data from adults.

- Measure the tibia, humerus, and radius bones, and the heights of several adults to the nearest half inch. Create a spreadsheet to organize the measurements. Use the formulas from Activity 2 in your spreadsheets to predict the heights of the adults.
- Compare the predicted heights with the measured heights. Does one of the formulas predict height better than the other formulas? Explain.

Finishing the Project

The answers to the four activities should help you complete your project. Assemble all the parts of your project in a folder. Include a summary of what you have learned about using the height formulas. What difficulties did you have? Are there ways to avoid these problems? What advice would you give to an archaeologist or forensic scientist about predicting heights from bone lengths?

Reflect and Revise

Ask a classmate to review your folder with you. Together, check that your graph is clearly labeled and accurate. Check that you have used formulas correctly and that your calculations are accurate. Is your spreadsheet well organized and easy to follow? Make any revisions necessary to improve your work.

Extending the Project

Archaeologists and forensic scientists use many other formulas related to the human body. Research formulas of this type by contacting your local police department or by searching the Internet.

Page 116

Chapter 2 Project Manager: The Big Dig!

Getting Started

Read the project. As you work on the project, you will need a calculator, a tape measure or ruler, and materials to make accurate and attractive graphs. Keep all of your work for the project in a folder.

Checklist

☐ Activity 1: organizing and analyzing data

☐ Activity 2: using formulas

☐ Activity 3: comparing male and female data

☐ Activity 4: comparing measurements

☐ project display

Suggestions

☐ Measure from the base of your thumb to the bend in your arm.

☐ Use the correct formulas for calculating your height. Try all three formulas to find the most accurate.

☐ Choose an effective table or graph.

☐ Include data from family members, teachers, or neighbors.

☐ Why might the measurements taken by another group differ? How accurate are these data? Do your graphs and spreadsheet(s) support your predictions?

Scoring Rubric

4   Appropriate types of graphs and charts are chosen. Graphs are labeled correctly and completely, and show accurate scales. Formulas and calculations are accurate. The spreadsheet presents data clearly and is easy to follow. Explanations are clear and correct.

3   The spreadsheet is complete and clear. The graph and formulas are appropriately chosen and used. There are minor errors in scale or computation. Reasoning and explanations are essentially correct, but sometimes awkward or unclear.

2   Graphs and selected formulas are somewhat correct. Calculations contain many errors. Explanations are not adequate.

1   Major elements of the project are incomplete or missing.

0   Project is not handed in or shows no effort.

Your Evaluation of Project Evaluate your work, based on the *Scoring Rubric.*

Teacher's Evaluation of Project